····· publisher's acknowledgements

We are excited to finally present this much-anticipa[...]e I *See: Learning Through Writing and Reflection*. It is with a[...]ve acknowledge the people who helped make this happen.

The first edition of *The Me I See* was born in 1998 out of our desire to provide a journaling/reflection tool for counselors and teachers to use with adolescents. It took on a life of its own and grew into a fun, "family" project that sparked our imaginations and inspired contributions from many of our friends, customers, authors, and employees—specifically, **Chris**, **Dave**, **Mony**, **Blu**, **Joshua**, **Mary**, **Kacie**, and **Matt**.

From the very beginning, *The Me I See* has been a collaboration of people looking within and sharing the questions of their hearts and lives—the questions that have kept them curious and motivated and centered. We turned those questions into prompts and placed them in a journaling format to help spark that same curiosity and insight in today's youth.

Chris Cavert has been a cheerleader for and contributor to *The Me I See* from its conception. **Susana Acosta Cavert** joined in and added her special touch to the process of putting this second edition together. Chris and Susana lent a great deal of time and energy to the maturing of this text, from submitting and organizing questions to proofing text and helping structure the approach of the content. They have been invaluable and are most appreciated. We hope they will always be on our team!

Carol Carlin, a contributing author of *Leading Together*, was one of many thoughtful and generous reviewers who influenced the final draft of the book. Carol went the extra mile by providing advice and giving us permission to pull from her experience as a teacher of journal writing. We thank Carol and all of our reviewers who gave so freely of their time. Their enthusiastic and constructive response reignited our desire to finish strong.

A small but invaluable group of interns also contributed to the project. Who better to help with prompts and the overall look, feel, and appeal of the book than those who would love having just such a book for themselves? **Madeleine Wiens**, **Aheren Richardson**, and **Joan Ranstrom** helped us make this book relevant, inviting, and personal. Their input, enthusiasm, and willingness to proof and proof again made them significant contributors and, in part, responsible for the success of this project.

Jen Stanchfield's enthusiasm for the original edition of *The Me I See* and her passion for engaging adolescents in the process of reflection made her the perfect choice to tap for providing some strong facilitation guidelines and suggestions to this second edition. In her usual generous and creative style, she added depth and width to the possibilities and potential of *The Me I See, 2nd Edition*. She has rounded out a great journaling book with her unique brand of "tips and tools." We thank Jen for helping us bring this project to fruition.

And as is the norm here, if not for **Ramona Cunningham**, there would be no book. Over time, her creative vision, determination, patience, and commitment has led to the quality of all Wood N Barnes books. However, this book is not only an example of her particular gifts, it is her particular gift to us. Mony planted the seed from which *The Me I See: Answering Life's Questions* grew and then carefully transplanted it. We thank her for inviting all of us to join in the adventure and promise that is *The Me I See: Learning Through Writing and Reflection*.

Finally, we freely admit that more people have contributed to this book than we can acknowledge. The comments and appreciation of the educators and students, counselors and clients who have used this book over the last decade have inspired its contents. **Thank you all for helping tremendously in the re-imagination, direction, and feel of the book.**

David Wood, Partner, Wood 'N' Barnes Publishing

The

me i see

2nd edition

Learning through writing and reflection

• • • • • • • • •

Wood 'N' Barnes Collective

Published by:

Wood 'N' Barnes Publishing
2309 N. Willow, Suite A, Bethany, OK
(405) 942-6812

Cover Art by Blue Designs
Copyediting & Layout Design by Ramona Cunningham
Photographs by Belinda Ranstrom
Special thanks to the Quincy High School 2008 Business Technology Students for participating in this project.

Printed in the United States of America
Bethany, Oklahoma
ISBN # 978-1-885473-74-5

. . . . . contents

The art of writing is the art of discovering what you believe.
Gustave Flaubert

When there are walls of ignorance between people,
when we don't know each other's stories,
we substitute our own myths about who that person is.
When we are operating with only a myth,
none of that person's truth will ever be known to us,
and we will injure them—mostly without ever meaning to.
Paula Lawrence Wehmiller

facilitation notes . . . .

Rest is much more than bodily relaxation.
Like a pause in the music, it affords the opportunity for one to catch up with what is going on.
Unknown

Our heavily scheduled, fast-paced society, filled with television, computers, and cell phones, does not lend itself to spending time in self-reflection. People don't often just sit down under a tree and think quietly, journal, or draw. Educators, counselors, therapists, group leaders, parents—all of us who choose to work with today's young people—are challenged by this reality. The practice of reflection is what helps us maintain balance in this hectic world. By passing the art of reflection on to our students and clients we are providing them with tools for thinking, exploring, and responding to the myriad of choices, decisions, and options they face every day.

Reflection helps people create purpose, meaning, and focus around the activities of their everyday lives. The educational philosopher John Dewey* stated that people do not truly learn from experiences until they reflect on them and decide how each experience is meaningful and relevant to their lives. Modern-day, brain-based research** supports this theory, validating the belief that taking the time for reflection and using a variety of different kinds of reflective techniques facilitates learning. This research and brain-compatible learning theory suggest that the practice of reflection is not just beneficial but necessary to the learning process.

One important benefit of engaging learners in the process of reflection is that it develops insight, which is an essential life skill, yet difficult to teach and learn. When educators and therapists intentionally engage students and clients in reflection activities, it encourages personal insight and recognition of skills, strengths, and goals. Reflective practice helps learners accept responsibility for learning and apply that learning to future situations. This formal recognition results in learners accessing their inner resources and calling on them when needed.

Journaling is a powerful reflection tool that helps individuals solidify and understand their thoughts and work through their personal feelings and reactions to the world around them. It stimulates creativity and gives the participants a tangible memoir of their experience and growth. *The Me I See* aims to provide an engaging and easy-to-use tool that will encourage these moments of self-reflection and a basic foundation whereby adolescents will recognize and come to value their own personal power, wisdom, and insight. It is meant not only to be a guide but also an inspiration to engage learners in the lifelong practice of journaling.

---

* Dewey, J. (1938). *Experience and education.* New York: Macmillan Publishing Co.
** Jensen, E. (2000). *Brain-based learning.* San Diego, CA: The Brain Store. Sousa, D. (2006). *How the brain learns.* Thousand Oaks, CA: Sage Publications.

What is *The Me I See?*

The Me I See is a simple, thorough collection of journaling prompts placed in an accessible workbook template. The pages are full of thought-provoking prompts in an inviting format with a sense of whimsy and fun that is far less intimidating than the blank page. These pages are conveniently reproducible and can be used alone or combined with photos and artwork to make writing fun, creative, and engaging.

The Me I See was designed to be used by educators, counselors, and therapists as a tool to help adolescents express themselves, reflect on their thoughts, feelings, and motivations, and explore the issues that shape their lives. The journaling exercises will help them learn about who they are as individuals. The exercises will give them some insights to cope with the stressors of being an adolescent and to interact positively with the world around them.

Educators will find *The Me I See* useful for engaging students in all kinds of classroom situations—from exploring issues and topics in health class, social curriculum, and peer leadership programs to English or Civics class. Therapists will find this tool valuable for helping adolescent clients work through their thoughts and emotions as they explore the cathartic aspect of journaling. *The Me I See* can also be the perfect supplement to group therapy sessions by providing opportunities for adolescents to engage in structured time alone, to reflect and process. This time away from the group balances and supports the group process. Individuals can reflect on topics that might not have come up during group discussion and explore thoughts they might not verbalize in a group setting.

How to Use *The Me I See*—Experiencing the Joy of Self-Reflection Through Writing

The original idea was to design a book/tool that could be used with adolescents in a variety of ways, and as the book took shape, the scope of possible uses grew. The book as a whole is for counselors and teachers to pull from—using the facilitation notes as a guide and reproducing prompt pages for client/student use. However, we have added a little flexibility by perforating the pages of the book. This makes it possible for teachers/counselors to remove facilitation notes, introductory chapter pages, any unneeded prompts, and so forth, turning the book into a personal journal that can be put in the hands of the student/client. The simple, open structure of *The Me I See* gives it great potential. We hope it will inspire you with all kinds of creative ideas. A few ideas for using the book as a whole or using individual reproducible pages from specific chapters include:

- Regular ongoing assignments as part of your curriculum to engage students in the practice of regular writing and reflection.

- As a supplement to coursework to review and reinforce content covered in class or group.

- To jump-start discussions in the classroom or group session.

- To track progress and growth throughout a program.

- For educators to gather feedback on what is working in the classroom or group. This alternative assessment tool can be used to review and reinforce content or lessons covered in class.

- As homework between individual or group counseling sessions to help clients reflect on their thoughts, feelings, and experiences, and to help them better articulate and explore treatment goals with their counselor or therapist.

- To identify goals, strengths, and resources and to map progress in treatment.

The book is organized by subject, starting with "the me I see" and progressing through subjects such as "values," "past," "family," and "social." Each subject area starts with lighter, easier-to-process prompts followed by more challenging ones. Choose the prompts that are appropriate for your class, group, or individual.

A list of additional prompts and blank, formatted pages are provided in the Make It Personal section starting on page 159. This makes it easy for you or the adolescents you work with to create personalized worksheets for specific lessons or topics. Just reproduce the format that appeals to you and fill in with your prompts.

The first page of each chapter suggests some ideas and guidelines for facilitating the journaling.

Consider providing a variety of tools for journaling, such as markers, crayons, other art supplies, collage materials—even a camera for photo journaling.

Some simple instructions for the end user entitled "Things for the Journal Writer to Consider" can be found on page 9. This can be used as a handout for the journalists or as an example of some encouraging words the facilitator can share with the journalists. It can also be left in the journal along with pages 7 and 8 to make this book into a personal journal for individual use.

Ethical Considerations—A Few Ground Rules for the Teacher, Counselor, or Group Facilitator to Consider

Warning: Some of the questions in *The Me I See* were designed for the counseling setting and the exploration of values and challenging social issues in leadership and civics groups. The questions might not be appropriate for every group and every setting. Know your group, and be thoughtful and intentional about the questions you use and your own abilities to manage and guide discussions that might come up in your groups. Keep in mind the extent of your training and remain within those bounds. The subjects for journal entries are intentionally designed to provoke thoughtfulness and intrapersonal reflection; use professional discretion when choosing entries for your adolescents to use in class or group. Remember that a student's writing might be a call for help.

Make sure participants in the school setting understand that confidentiality cannot be guaranteed. And be cognizant of your school's or agency's policy on confidentiality and student writing/artwork before you introduce this type of assignment to students. Be intentional about how the journals or journal pages will be used. In the academic setting where reflective writing is part of ongoing coursework, carefully consider how or if you are going to assess or grade these reflective writings, and then be clear with students about your expectations. We suggest, in the context of this book, grading for completion rather than content or grammar.

Establish some ground rules and clarification for participants on how the answers to questions will or will not be shared between student and teacher, counselor and client, or among peers. It can be very powerful but sometimes daunting for writers to share their work. As facilitator, prepare for the sensitive nature of, and possible risk involved in, sharing one's innermost thoughts and feelings by helping your group establish some positive group norms around what and how work is shared (see page 5). Whether you are sharing one on one as counselor and client, or having students share journals with peers, help create and maintain a space in which everyone feels emotionally safe and comfortable, and where feedback and reactions will be constructive and useful.

As a facilitator, you want to ensure that the following understandings, behaviors, and qualities are present in a group before participants engage in sharing their journals:

- Clear goals and expectations about why and how information from journals will be shared.

- Students demonstrate a capacity to trust and be trusted by other group members.

- Respect for privacy is understood—"What is shared in group, stays in group," unless someone is at risk to themselves or others. Make participants aware that anything indicating harm to self or others will need to be addressed. In the classroom setting, students need to expect that what is written as part of school assignments will likely be seen by the teacher. Remind students that reflective writing in school is different than private journaling, as school is a public place and journal sheets could be lost or left behind in class.

- If reflective writing is going to be shared in group/class, participants need to have some choice and control about what they share with the group and have the option to pass.

- Participants need to have a clear understanding about any grading requirements/ expectations before they start.

Note: Two resources for creating a positive environment for learning, sharing and building community are *Journey Toward the Caring Classroom* by Laurie Frank and *Tips & Tools: The Art of Experiential Group Facilitation* by Jennifer Stanchfield (see resources on page 185).

If you are going to share work in a classroom or group setting, guide the group in creating its own agreement about the ground rules for sharing. This can be done by brainstorming a list or agreement (see some great ideas to start this process on page 6). The following are some possible ground rules for sharing:

- What is shared in group, stays in group (unless a safety issue arises).
- Use positive, supportive language.
- Believe in the best intentions of others.
- No judgements.
- Share only what you are comfortable sharing.
- Be honest.
- No sarcasm.
- Be fully present when listening to others share.

When sharing journals in a group setting it helps to build comfort, trust, and confidence by starting with pairs and then moving to dyads before discussing with the larger group. Another effective way to make sharing with the group more comfortable for participants is to begin by inviting the writers to share something they particularly liked about their writing or ask for specific feedback they would like to have from the group.

If participants are intimidated or struggling with the blank page (even with a prompt), consider introducing this simple, creative, reflective process excerpted from Carol Carlin's *Journaling as an Academic Tool* coursework:

- Relax: The two keys are to eliminate visual stimuli and increase oxygen. Hence, close your eyes and take deep breaths. Clear your mind.

- Visualization: With eyes closed and staying in the relaxed state, visualize the topic by calling on the senses. What do you see? What are the colors? What do you hear? Are there certain smells? What are the pictures in your mind? and so forth.

- Brainstorm: (Participants may need to be introduced to some brainstorming techniques such as listing, clusters, free writing.) Spend some time brainstorming and then record your ideas.

- Draft: Select part of the material from the brainstorm for inclusion in responding to the prompt.

Carol also suggests that, by defining a journal as a recorded observation, you open the door to anything goes, and take the focus off making sure everything is grammatically correct. There is a time for editing and perfection, but I prefer to use journaling as a time for exploring ideas and suggesting growth.

Establishing Positive Group Norms*

Group norms are the values and characteristics that exist in every group. They include a code of conduct, acceptable behaviors or customs, habits, and expectations about how things will be done. Group norms influence how group members communicate and work together. When a group intentionally works together to agree on clarifying and establishing norms that all members can endorse, the group becomes stronger, more effective, and more aware of its dynamics and behavior. The process of establishing the norms can become a team-building activity in itself. When facilitating this process remember that these norms will change and need to be clarified throughout the group process. **Establishing group norms is a process, not an event.**

The first meeting, first day, or first hour (depending on the length of time the group will meet) is not likely to be an appropriate time to create meaningful or relevant agreements. After the group has had some time together, this process becomes more authentic and most effective. Combined with reflective practice and regular feedback and evaluation, it becomes a meaningful and useful tool for the group. Helping the group create behavioral norms regarding comments and judgments during group activities and discussions increases the amount of sharing and interaction and enhances the depth of group experience.

Facilitators are often stymied by the idea of a boring contract or list of rules. This barrier is lifted when one thinks of this activity not as "housekeeping," but as an interesting and engaging activity that can involve different mediums. By presenting the group norms agreement task in different ways—combining list making, artwork, using props, and discussion—it becomes a richer, more significant, and memorable experience.

The idea of valuing the experience does not require that participants be best friends with everyone in their classroom, work group, or program. Ideally, group members come to recognize that they and their peers have value and can offer important contributions to the group experience. If students appreciate the experience and value the group (both others and themselves), they end up with a more "valuable" outcome. A facilitator can help a group define norms in many ways. I usually start this ongoing group process with simple list making and discussion. As the group develops, artwork and symbols become effective.

---

* This information on establishing group norms is excerpted from Jennifer Stanchfield's *Tips & Tools: The Art of Experiential Group Facilitation*, © 2007, Wood 'N' Barnes Publishing.

In the context of using this book with a group, we recommend first and foremost carefully sequencing sharing activities. **Trust within a group and comfort with the process is built incrementally.** Remember to start the process of sharing writing by breaking into pairs or dyads, thus helping participants work up to the process of sharing with the large group. Also remember to start by asking for volunteers who want to share their work. It is key that from the beginning, you as facilitator establish the norm that they have a choice about what they share with the group.

To discuss norms around sharing and giving and receiving feedback, ask group members what they want to experience personally and as a group when sharing takes place.

Some great ideas to start to this process:

Have the group brainstorm a list with two columns. Ask them to decide what behaviors are acceptable and unacceptable when sharing and working together as a group. Write the acceptable behaviors in the "In" column and the unacceptable behaviors in the "Out" column. Or, label your columns "Us"/"Not Us." Revisit these lists from time to time as needed.

"In" Behaviors	"Out" Behaviors	"Us"	"Not Us"

Many facilitators have had success using artwork. In group norms agreements around sharing, have the group create a symbol representing their sharing circle or classroom and fill the circle with words or pictures of what behaviors they want to see in the group and outside of the circle place what's not okay, or what they don't want to have present in their group. Eventually you might come to the point where you could ceremoniously cut away the not okay drawings or list to demonstrate that when we focus on the positive norms often the negative falls away on its own. For more ideas visit our resources page.

A Final Note:

Remember to take time to look at the facilitation notes we have provided on the first page of each chapter. You will find information for using specific prompts to enhance learning in that area, some specific ideas for creating a positive environment, and suggestions for artistic materials to spark interest and creativity.

The Me I See has been a fun and thought-provoking project to put together. We hope it inspires you to engage those you work with in the practice of journaling. We believe it is a powerful tool that can enhance your program outcomes and encourage individuals to take responsibility for their learning and growth. Regardless of the specific setting, *The Me I See* can become a transformative gift for the users, empowering them with self-knowledge, giving them the confidence to share what's on their minds, and, in fact, revealing that they are the authors of their own lives.

Jen Stanchfield
Ramona Cunningham
June, 2012

. . . . . . if found
please return to . . . .

_____
name

_____
contact information

Additional information...

This is what I would say to an uninvited person reading this book...

My support network includes...   contact information...

Here is a place to list your personal support network (people/resources you can depend on)—this could include family members, teachers, school counselors, pastors, youth support agencies, etc.

things for the journal writer to consider

Everyone has a story. Our life stories help us understand where we are now and help lead us to the paths we might choose in the future. This book is designed to be a place to tell your story by exploring your thoughts, emotions, views of the world around you, and future goals and dreams. Make this book work for you. As you answer the questions take your time, find a quiet space, and enjoy the process of focusing just on you and your thoughts. Be honest and true to yourself, your beliefs, opinions, and goals.

Challenge yourself to respond to the difficult prompts and go a little deeper on the topics you can answer easily. Recording your thoughts and reflecting on your experiences and what is important to you will help you tap into your own personal power and wisdom. It will help you understand and reinforce your strengths and identify areas you might need to work on. The practice of reflective writing will help you define and focus on what you want in life. Look at this as a gift to yourself—a lasting record of your personal growth and change.

Be creative in approaching these pages, and throw in some personality. Record your thoughts with words, drawings, pictures from magazines, photographs, or other artwork.

You are the author:

- If a prompt in *The Me I See* doesn't fit you, change it to fit your life experiences.

- If you find a topic difficult to write about, give it some time and come back to it later. If you are still stuck, ask for some input from someone close to you.

- Make up your own prompts. There are blank pages in the back of the book for you to fill in any way that suits you.

Enjoy telling your story, revisiting your past, and exploring the places the future might take you....

Follow effective action with quiet reflection.
From the quiet reflection will come even more effective action.
Peter Drucker

the me I see

There is only one of you in the world, just one.
And if that is not fulfilled, then something has been lost.
~Martha Graham

Chapter was designed to introduce adolescents to the practice of journaling. This chapter begins with simple, playful prompts focused on personal interests, favorite foods, movies, and activities. As students/clients become familiar and comfortable with expressing themselves on paper, the prompts move to engaging them in reflecting on their emotions and perceptions of themselves.

- Encourage the process of self-reflection by providing a comfortable environment.

- Remember to discuss if and how the answers will be shared, as well as acceptable/ unacceptable responses to the sharing.

- Build trust and confidence by moving into the sharing process slowly. Start with personal reflection time, moving into pair-share or small groups as you sense the group is ready.

- If you decide to facilitate sharing prompts with the larger group, guide participants in setting ground rules for sharing (see Facilitation Notes).

- Many of the introductory prompts are ideal for warm-up activities and icebreakers with large groups.

- Remember to help inspire creativity and engagement by providing art supplies and collage materials to supplement the writing.

I enjoy collecting...

Some things that always make me smile are...

My favorite foods are...

I enjoy collecting...

I enjoy stories about...

My favorite day of the week is...   because...

My favorite time of day is... because...

At this point in my life, I could write a book about...

These are some "fun facts" about me...

My favorite books so far include...   because...

My favorite kind of entertainment is...   because...

I am most like this actor/ actress... because...

I think a good movie should include...

I would walk out of a movie if...

My picture should be in the dictionary as an example of the word...   because...

If I had my own magazine, it would be called...

An inside story about me would be...

If I went into business for myself,
it would be... because...

To stay healthy, I...

For exercise, I like to...

- - - - - - - - - - - - - - - - - - - -
- - - - - - - - - - - - - - - - - - - -
- - - - - - - - - - - - - - - - - - - -
- - - - - - - - - - - - - - - - - - - -
- - - - - - - - - - - - - - - - - - - -
- - - - - - - - - - - - - - - - - - - -
- - - - - - - - - - - - - - - - - - - -
- - - - - - - - - - - - - - - - - - - -
- - - - - - - - - - - - - - - - - - - -
- - - - - - - - - - - - - - - - - - - -
- - - - - - - - - - - - - - - - - - - -
- - - - - - - - - - - - - - - - - - - -
- - - - - - - - - - - - - - - - - - - -
- - - - - - - - - - - - - - - - - - - -

My favorite things to do on a rainy day are...

Some of my personal habits that people may find a little strange...

Some habits I would really like to break are...   because...

If I continue to live with my existing habits, I can expect...

When I look in the mirror and see my reflection, I...

This is how I would describe my personality...

My experience with judging/being judged by looks...

Some of my favorite poetry is... because...

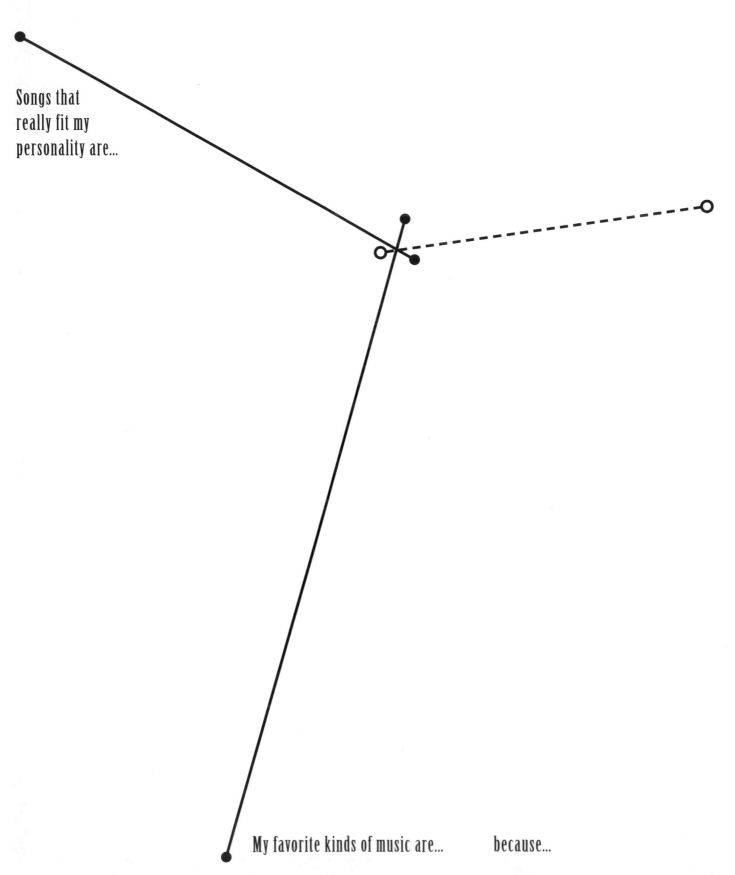

Songs that
really fit my
personality are...

My favorite kinds of music are...   because...

The best ideas I've had so far include...

I have always wanted to...

I would really like to learn more about...   and this is how I could do it...

If I had three wishes...

I would/would not like to change
my name because...

This is what you would learn about me
by looking in my closet...

The "official rules" of my life include...

This is how I would describe my personal appearance...

My personal motto is...   because...

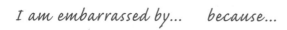

I am embarrassed by...   because...

Sometimes
I wonder...

I always think it's funny when...

Things in nature that have special meaning to me are...
because...

My
favorite
work of art is...
because...

The most
inspirational
thing that has ever
happened to me was...

Some things that I will not tolerate are...

Based on my life experience, "Sticks and stones may break my bones, but words..."

This is how I handle criticism...

When other people cry, I...   **because...**

My personal experience around giving a person a second chance...

This is how I handle compliments...

If my life was a
MOVIE
this is who would be in the credits & what their job was...

Starring?

Costarring?

Directors?

Cast?

Crew?

Script?

Producer?

Music?

Make-up?

Hair?

Costumes?

Catered by...

Things I like about myself are ••••••• ....

•••• ••• •••• ••• •••• •••• •••• ••••••••••••••••••••••••••••

Things about myself I'd like to change are •••••• ....

My greatest accomplishments so far... | **& how they make me feel...**

10 things that make me happy are...

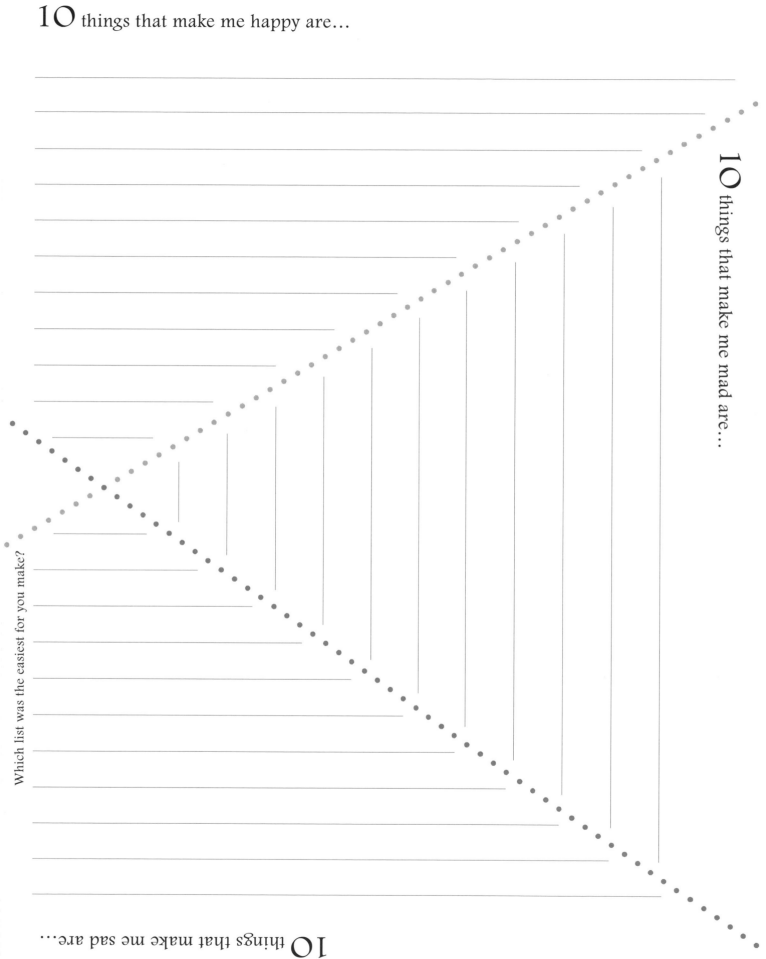

10 things that make me mad are...

10 things that make me sad are...

Which list was the easiest for you make?

Design a T-shirt with a message that expresses your normal Monday mood.

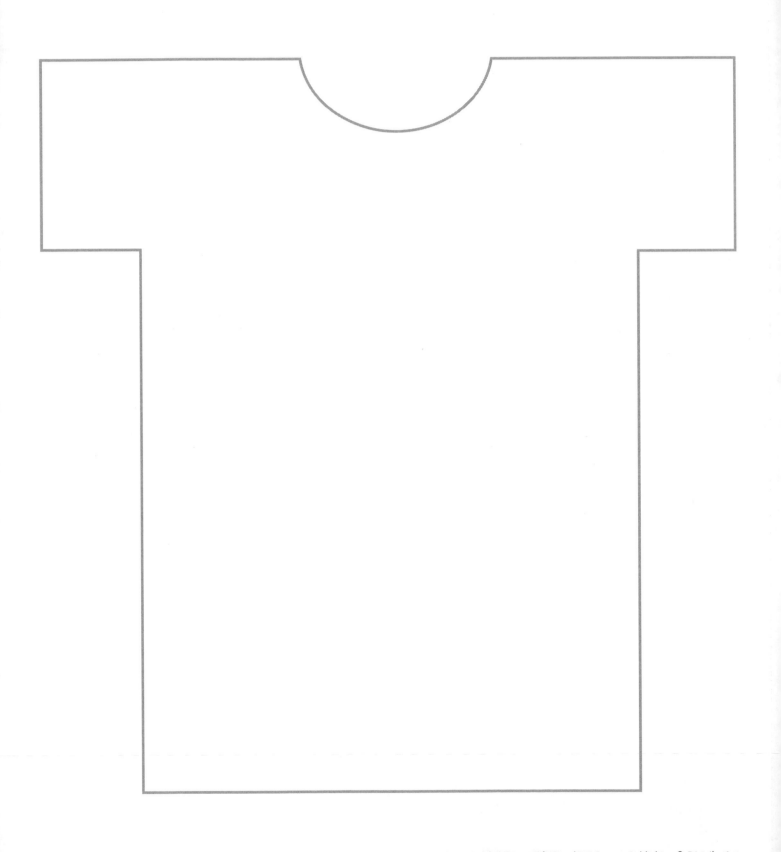

Sometimes I have to stand on my head to see things as they are, when the world seems so upside-down, that is the only position in which anything makes sense.
~**Martha Graham**

This chapter gives adolescents an opportunity to reflect on what is important to them and on their beliefs and feelings about the choices they make. Participants may find they have opinions they are not even aware of—just below the surface, waiting to come out.

Be observant. If you sense that any participants are struggling with an issue that arises out of the prompts or discussion, give them some one-on-one time or encourage them to seek help from a guidance counselor or other appropriate professional. The prompts on page 36 can be used to help your students know where and how to find school and community resources available to them. Encourage them to research available resources and use them to make informed decisions.

- Remind adolescents to carefully consider the prompts, take time to reflect, and be honest.

- If they find a prompt too difficult to answer, invite them to come back to it later.

- If a prompt doesn't fit their life, have individuals adjust it to fit their particular situation.

- Introduce your students to the notion of being a change agent. "I can be a change agent, even though I'm not perfect and haven't yet arrived."

- There may be specific topics around values that you want to expand on further or are a better fit with your current program. Using the blank pages provided in the Make It Personal section (page 159), choose prompts from the Additional Prompts (page 175) or create your own questions to fit specific individual or group needs.

- Invite your students/clients to make up a page of prompts that they would like to see discussed in class/group.

The most difficult decision I made recently was...

A time I put myself at risk to help others was...

I have been raised to believe in...

This is how my dreams influence my life...

If I could have one day to myself to do anything I wanted, I would...

I would like to hold the world's record in...

because...

because...

When faced with a difficult decision, I talk to...   because...

Some helpful resources in my community that teens should be aware of are...   because...

Some personal situations I have been in where I needed outside help were...

My most valued possessions are...
because...

I know I have too much stuff when...

I deal with it by...

I would honestly be willing to give up all my possessions for... because...

If I could trade places with someone over the age of 24, it would be...   because...

This is the kind of adult I would like to become...

I think adults in general are...   because...

This is how my beliefs are
different than my friends...

I learned the difference between right and
wrong from...

I think the difference between tolerance and
acceptance is...

My power comes from...   because...

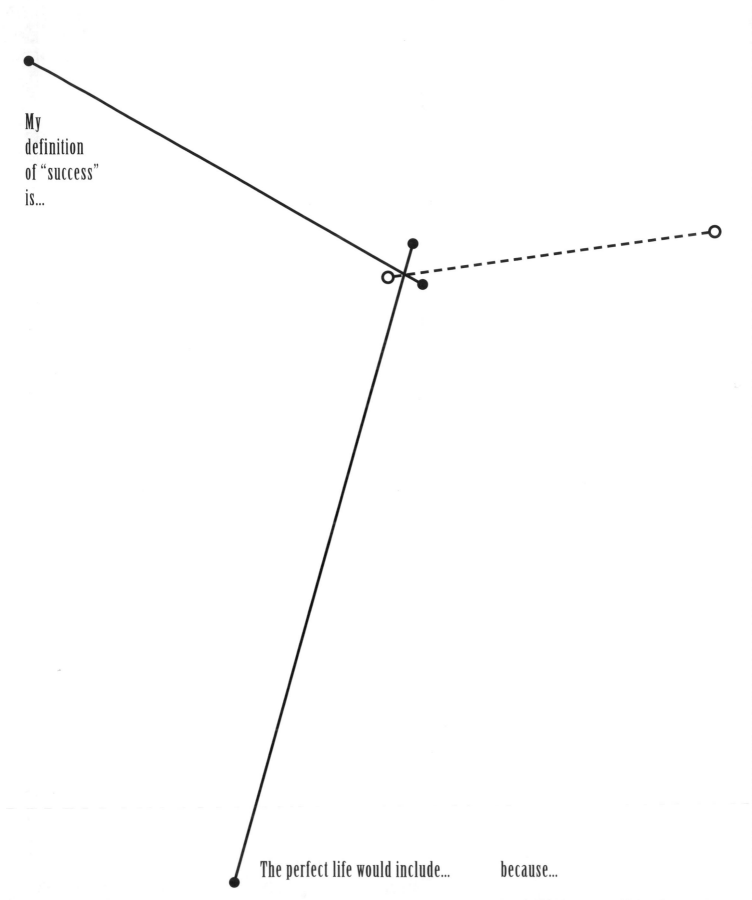

My
definition
of "success"
is...

The perfect life would include...   because...

My thoughts about money are...   because...

If I had a million dollars to give away...

I am saving money for...   because...

The nationalities that are part of my heritage include...
and this is how I feel about it...

Some things I take personally are...   because...

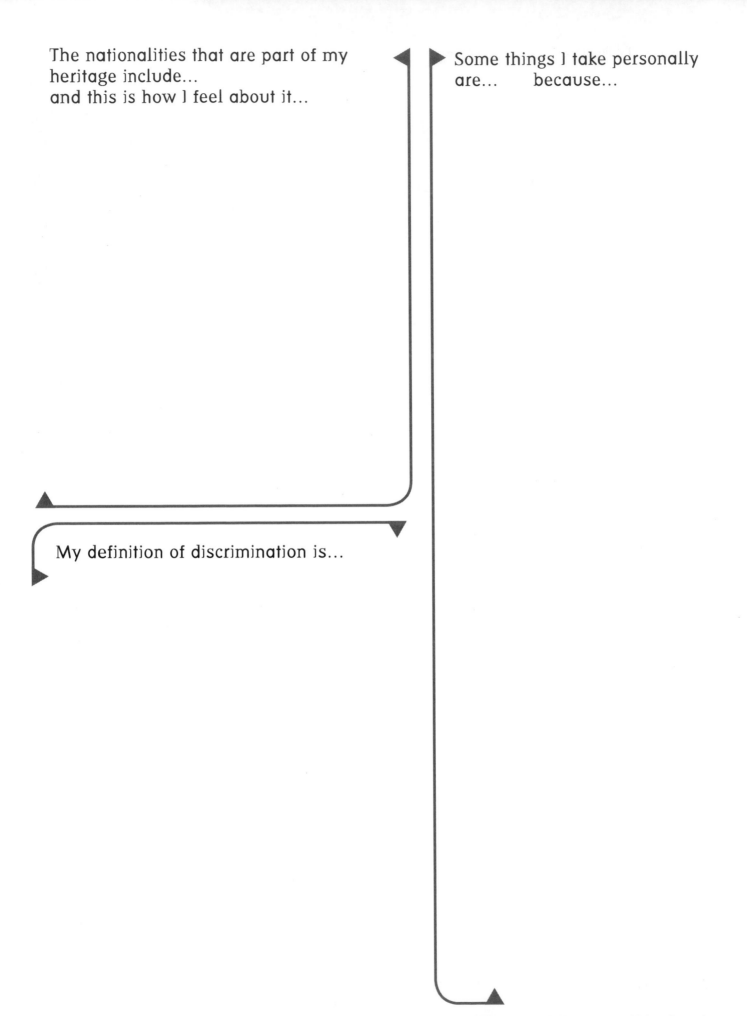

My definition of discrimination is...

My spiritual beliefs are...
because...

These are the religions I would like
to know more about... because...

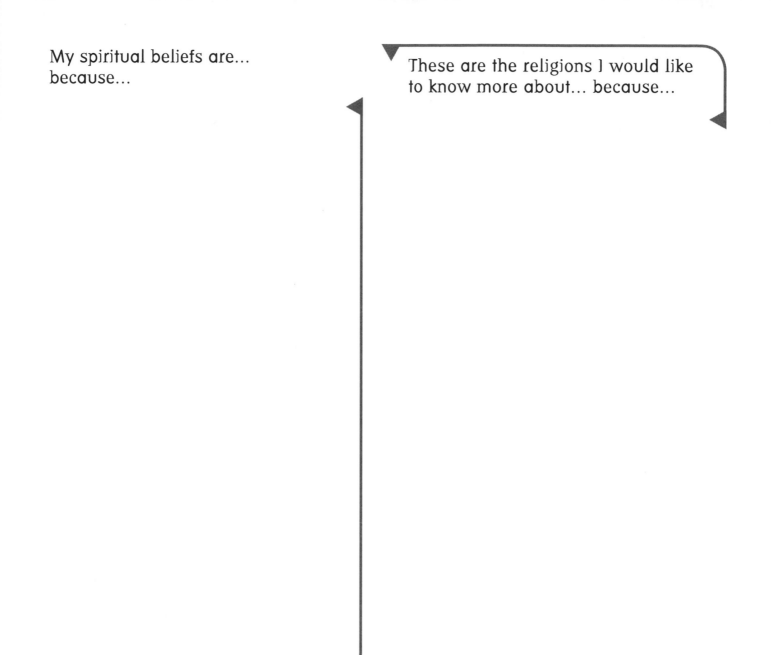

My definition of a "miracle" is...   because...

In my opinion, some things that can ruin a
person's reputation are...

because...

This is how I
feel about lying...

Some things I've done that I regret... and the lessons I learned...

Things I believe in that help me make sense of life are...

To me,
one of life's
great mysteries is...
because...

Something that
has a big impact on
my life is... because...

What I value most...   why...

my creed or philosophy...

_____ _____
signature   date

This is what I would do with a million dollars ...

views

3

The right to be heard does not automatically include the right to be taken seriously.
~Hubert Humphrey

Chapter three provides prompts to help adolescents reflect on their views of the world, covering everything from the media, popular culture, and the Internet to social and political issues.

- Use the prompts in this chapter to initiate a break-out session of group sharing of journaling. Through the process of group discussion, adolescents have the opportunity to broaden their perspective and learn to accept different points of view.

- This is a great place to explore the impact of peer pressure and the concept of empathy and respect for differences. Remind adolescents that it is okay to disagree. In fact, different beliefs and values provide richness.

- Creating group norms for sharing in group or class is especially important if you choose to facilitate a discussion group around the prompts in this chapter (see pages 5–6).

- This chapter lends itself to using photo journaling and artwork as an alternative to the written word. The prompts on Internet, popular culture, and news present an opportunity to blend in photographs, drawings, and collage/found items to help individuals communicate their viewpoints. Increase involvement and fun by having magazines and art materials on hand and encouraging the use of photos, video, and music—this could grow into a class documentary project!

I choose to/not to have my own personal space on the Internet because...

The Internet has influenced my life in these ways...

If the Internet no longer existed...

I think the best ways to communicate are... because...

My thoughts on texting are...

My advice for making friends through the Internet is...

because...

because...

My thoughts on our political system are...   because...

Some causes I think are worth supporting are...   because...

I believe one of the greatest world leaders is/was...   because...

I can make a difference in my community by...

If I had a talk show, this is a list of who I would want to interview... because...

- -
- -
- -
- -
- -
- -
- -
- -
- -
- -
- -
- -
- -
- -
- -

My personal experience with doing volunteer work is...

Things I recycle on a regular basis are...   because...

These are some of my concerns about our planet...

My personal efforts toward taking care of our world include...

My favorite/least favorite fashion styles are...   because...

My thoughts on body piercing and permanent tattoos...

Some ways the media/advertising has influenced my friends and me...

When I want to know what is happening in the world, I...

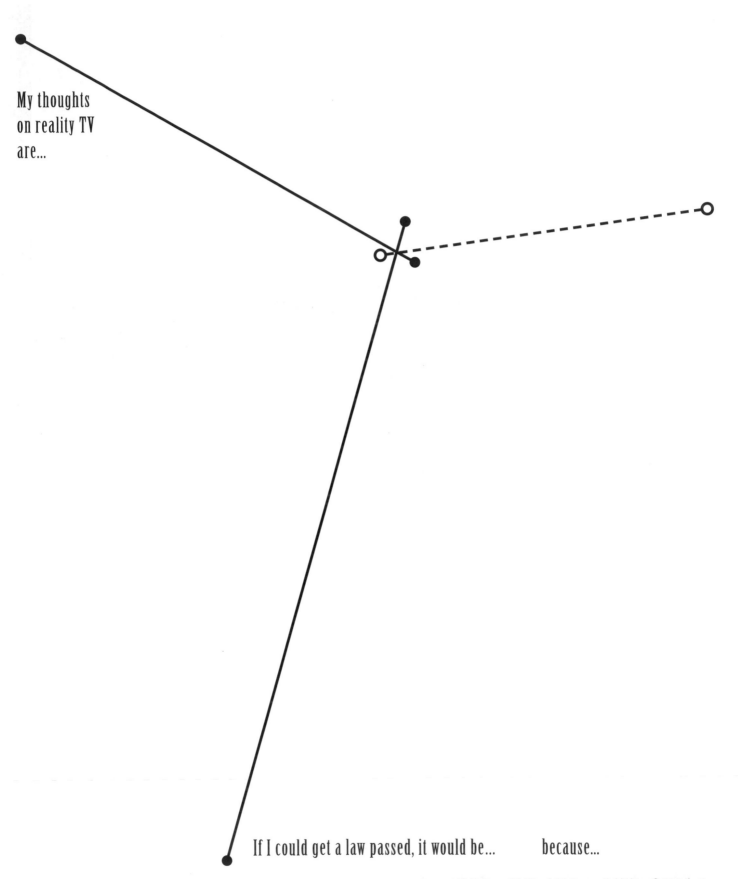

My thoughts
on reality TV
are...

If I could get a law passed, it would be...   because...

I think I would/would not be a good role model to a younger person because...

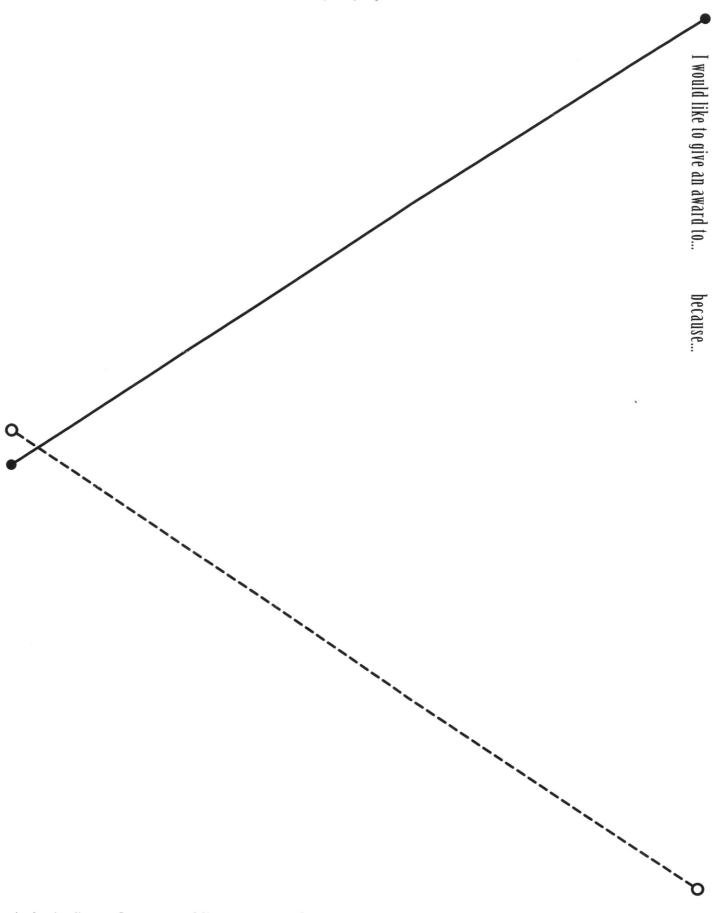

I would like to give an award to...   because...

Authority figures I respect and listen to are...   because...

All children should have...

My personal experience with racism or stereotyping has taught me...   because...

This is how I would like to be treated when I am old...

The most important things I do now to positively influence my future are...

The top three priorities in my life are...   because...

Some random acts of kindness I like to practice are...

My description of a good leader ❖ ❖ ❖

❖

Create an ad about a social issue you feel passionate about.

My idea of a perfect community is…

family

4

Call it a clan, call it a network, call it a tribe, call it a family.
Whatever you call it, whoever you are, you need one.
~Jane Howard

This chapter helps adolescents reflect on their concept of "family," family experiences, the "ideal" family, and hopes for future family life. It is important to be cognizant of the different concepts of family that exist within your group as you facilitate reflection and discussion on this topic.

- In most cases, we have put the word family or parent in quotes. Remind your group that "family" means different things to different people. Any definition of family applies to the prompts in this chapter. Ask your adolescents to make the prompts fit their particular circumstances.

- Use the first two pages of prompts in this chapter to help your group explore different kinds of families: single-parent families, children who live with grandparents or other extended family members, adoptive/foster families, and so forth. The Family Portrait prompt on page 64 could be a great place to start—be sure to provide art and collage materials.

- Again, be observant—if you sense that any participants are struggling with an issue that arises out of the prompts or discussion, give them some one-on-one time or encourage them to seek help from a guidance counselor or other appropriate professional. Be sensitive about loss and unusual circumstances. Some adolescents might not live with their family. Some may have lost a parent or have a parent away because of work, military service, or incarceration. Adolescents might be dividing their time between two families due to divorce or separation. This list could go on and on.

Note: Prompts that we identified as appropriate for the classroom setting are formatted in this chapter. Prompts that explore deeper feelings about family life are listed on page 178. Using the blank pages from the Make It Personal section (page 159) you can explore family-related topics further and create journal pages appropriate for your client.

My "Family" Portrait

My definition of the word "family" is...

A basic description of my "family" would be...

Some characteristics that make my "family" different than others would include...

Things I enjoy doing with my "family" are...   because...

We laugh the most as a "family" when we...

My best early-childhood memories are...

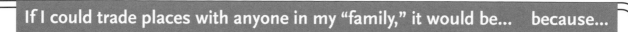

If I could trade places with anyone in my "family," it would be...   because...

If I had to choose another "family" to live with, it would be...

If I could add anyone to my "family," it would be...

because...

because...

My description of the perfect parent is...

My "family's" general attitude toward me seems to be...

- -

- -

- -

- -

- -

- -

- -

- -

The fairy tale that my "family" brings to mind is... because...

Some things I would like to say to my
"family"...

My "family" would be closer if...

A typical morning at my house includes...

Family traditions that I enjoy the most are...

These are my thoughts on how families should make decisions...

Some ways that I get attention from my "family"...

The most encouraging thing anyone in my "family" has ever said to/done for me...

A "family" member who has impacted my life the most is...   because...

This is a description of a "family" photograph I would always like to keep...

The general
atmosphere
in my house is...

Some smells that remind me of home are...

Some things I would really like to hear from my "family" are...

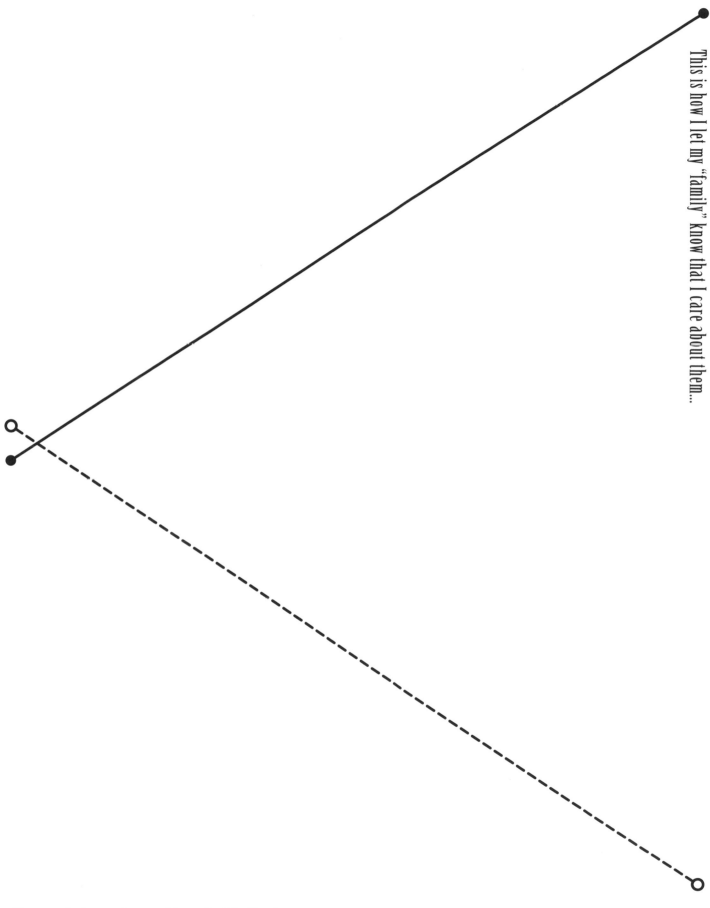

This is how I let my "family" know that I care about them...

The worst circumstances I have had to live in...

This is a list of my "family" responsibilities... | **& how they make me feel...**

If my family was a sandwich,

Here is what ingredient each of us would be... because...

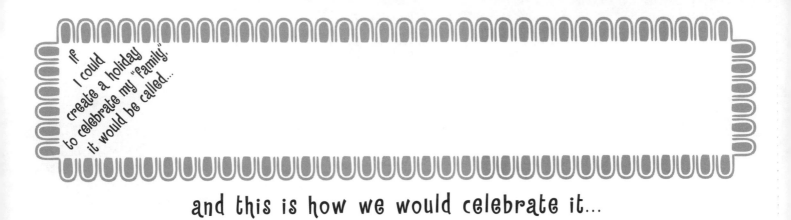

If I could create a holiday to celebrate my "family," it would be called...

and this is how we would celebrate it...

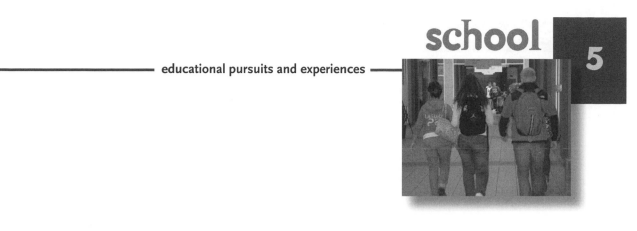

Education is not the filling of a pail, but the lighting of a fire.
~W. B. Yeats

Chapter five allows students to explore and share their school experiences. Most teens spend the majority of their time in school or school-related activities. This is an opportunity for educators to learn more about what is "really" going on in school from the student's perspective. Be aware that you might need to develop a "thick skin," and learn not to take it personally as students share their honest opinions about school and education. This information can be invaluable in helping you and your adolescents create positive change in your school and learn about what is working and not working in your own classroom.

- As with other subjects explored in *The Me I See*, establish group norms for how information is shared in the classroom, from student to student and teacher to student.

- Address specific school topics and classroom goals by using the blank pages provided in the Make It Personal section (page 159). Choose prompts from the list of Additional Prompts (page 175) or create your own.

- Invite your student/client to make up a page of prompts that they would like to see discussed in class/group.

The perfect education would include...

The class I've enjoyed the most so far is...

because...

One of my favorite school memories is...

This is a description of my all-time favorite teacher...

Some advice I'd like to give to educators is...

A report card that I would like to give to a past teacher is...   because...

The best encouragement I've received from a teacher was...   because...

These are my thoughts about trying to excel academically, work a part-time job, and/or participate in extracurricular activities...

One of my most embarrassing moments in school was...

I study best under these conditions...

When I get stressed over grades or deadlines, I...

The things about school that feel the most rewarding to me are... because...

My definition of "school spirit" is...   because...

My favorite extracurricular activities are...   because...

Three ways I could help make our school a better place...

This is how I feel about sharing
homework with friends...
because...

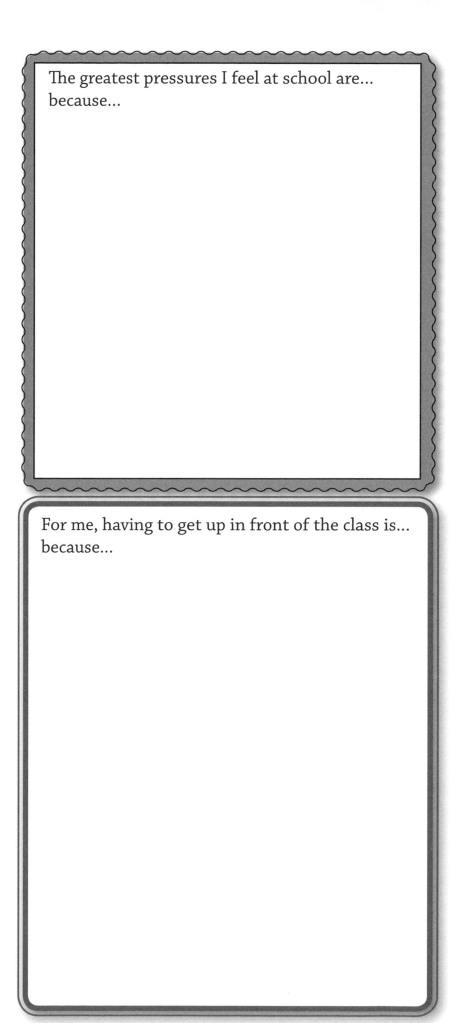

The greatest pressures I feel at school are...
because...

For me, having to get up in front of the class is...
because...

When I need help at school, I know I can count on...   because...

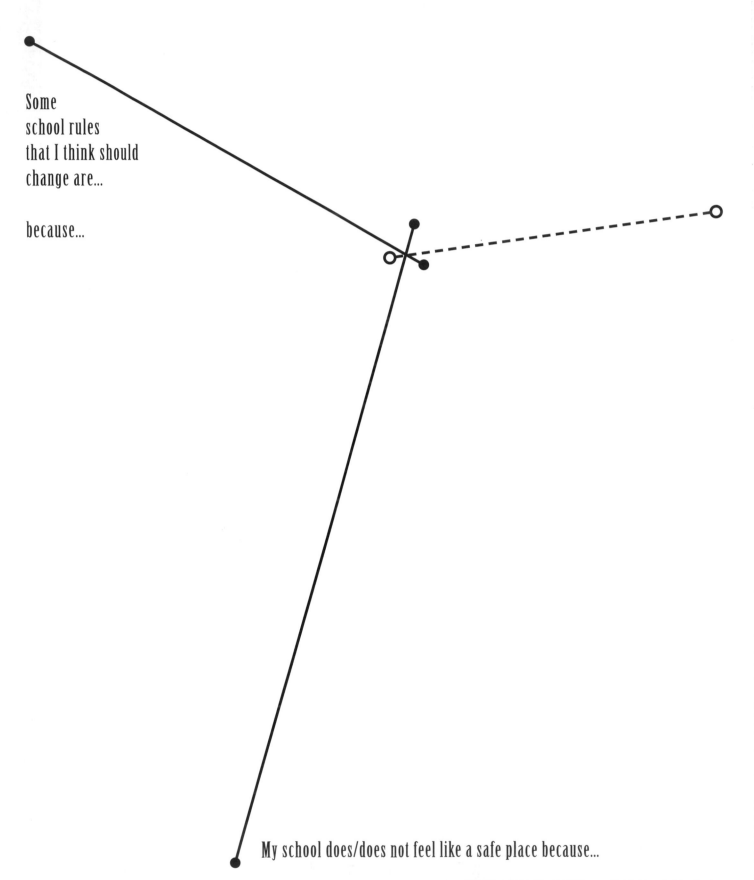

Some
school rules
that I think should
change are...

because...

My school does/does not feel like a safe place because...

Some things I have learned at school that I know will help me in life are...
because...

My personal experience with teasing and bullying in my school...

Things that distract me from paying attention in class are...

When I think about going to college, I...
because...

Some things I would be good at teaching others are...
because...

My thoughts about furthering my education by joining the military are...
because...

Some things I would like to see happen for me before the end of the school year are...

When I graduate from high school, I plan to...

I am considering furthering my education by...

This is what I think about the role of sports in school...

My personal thoughts on prayer (or some form of prayer) in school are...   because...

My thoughts on home schooling are... because...

I would/would not like to participate in a foreign exchange student program because...

If I could choose to participate in an internship as part of my schooling, it would be...   because...

I see high school graduation more as an ending/beginning because...

THIS IS HOW I WOULD REARRANGE MY HOMEROOM CLASSROOM.

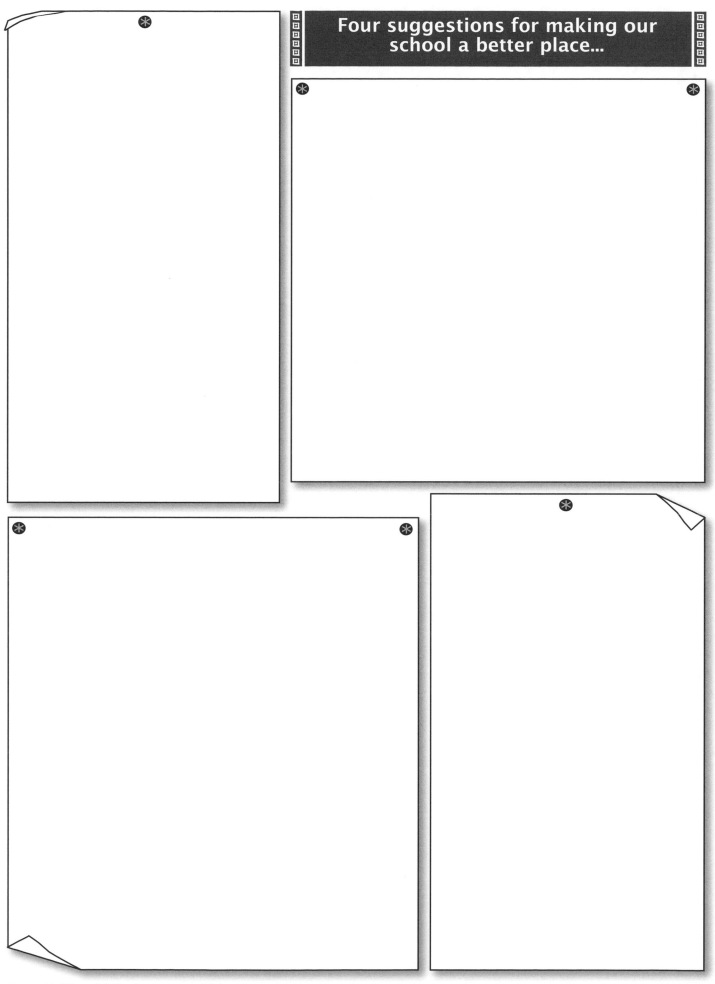

Four suggestions for making our school a better place...

This is the message I would paint on the wall of a hallway in my school to inspire future students...

social

6

*Remember that as a teenager you are at the last stage of your life
when you will be happy to hear that the phone is for you.*
~Fran Lebowitz

The opinions and approval of peers often eclipse what family thinks as adolescents begin to broaden their world. The adolescent years are filled with learning how to step out socially, interact in relationships, choose friends, and cope with peer pressure. The prompts in this chapter explore the influence that friends have, how friends are chosen, and their own influence on others.

- This is another chapter that lends itself to meaningful group discussions around social norms, relationships, leadership, and peer pressure.

- These prompts are appropriate for leadership and peer mentor programs. A great model for using reflection questions in an ongoing teen/peer mentorship program is *Open to Outcome* by Micah Jacobson and Mari Ruddy.

- Use the blank pages in the Make It Personal section (page 159) for adolescents to write some of their own questions about relationships, peers, and social life.

- And remember to help inspire creativity and engagement by providing art supplies and collage materials to supplement the writing. Making a friends/class photo journal could be a fun project.

These are the qualities I look for in a friend...

When I have good news, the first person I want to share it with is...

and my favorite way to share is...

My favorite places to just hang out are...   because...

People seem to like me because...

The people I am most comfortable around are...

because...

The type of person I have trouble getting along with is...

because...

The first thing I notice about another person is...   this tells me...

I think my friends like me because...

- -

- -

- -

- -

- -

- -

- -

Someone I would really like to spend time with is... because...

Some boundaries I have learned to set in my relationships are...   because...

_____

If I found out that a friend was lying to me, I would...

I think the best way to end a relationship is...   because...

Some of my favorite things to do with friends are...

I am inclusive/exclusive when it comes to friends because...

My personal experience with cliques is...

This is how I see social networking (Facebook, Youtube, Twitter, etc.) affecting my relationships...

Some of the ways my friends influence me are... because...

My personal experience with gossiping is...

My personal opinion about teasing or being teased is...

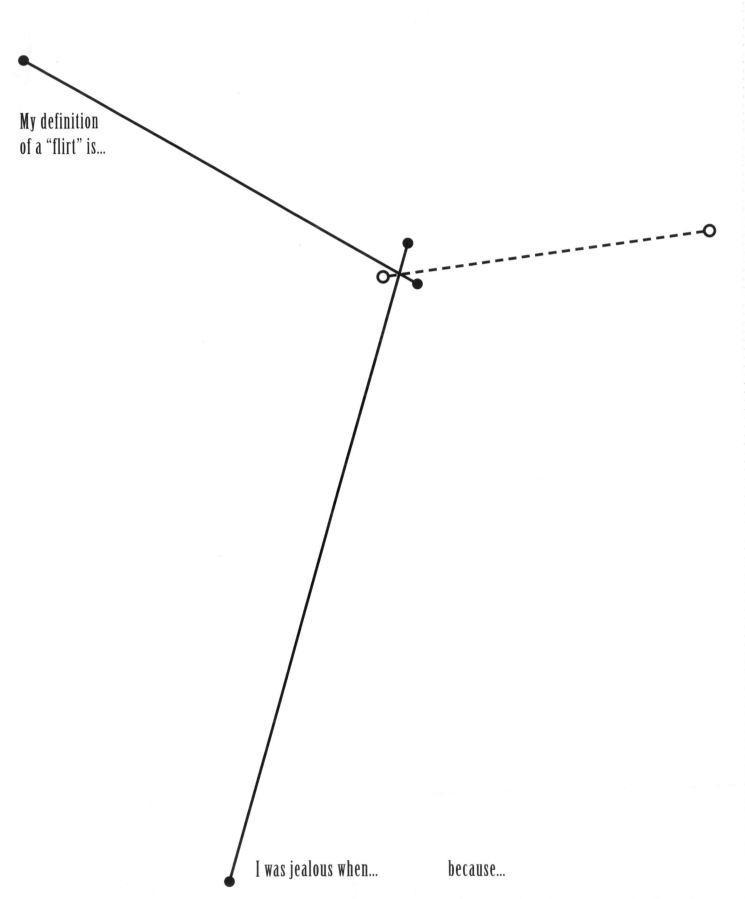

My definition
of a "flirt" is...

I was jealous when...   because...

A really rotten thing I did to someone else was...   this is how I feel about it now...

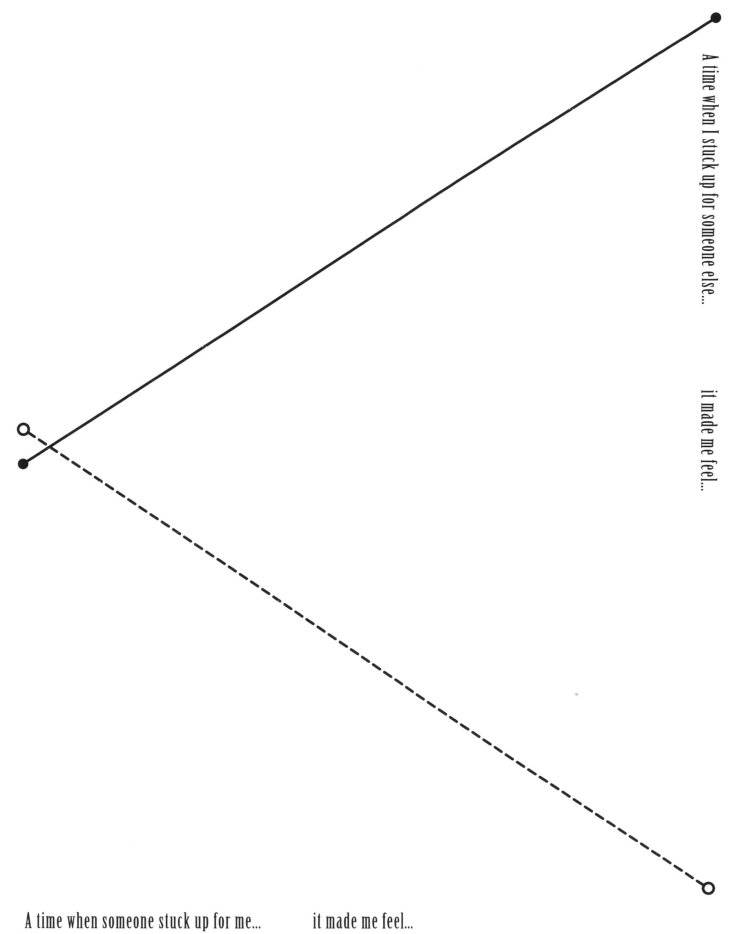

A time when I stuck up for someone else...

it made me feel...

A time when someone stuck up for me...   it made me feel...

If a friend asked for money, I would...

If I suspected that my friend was going through a hard time, I would...
because...

When a friend and I disagree, I...
because...

A friend that I have now, that I hope to always be close to is... because...

A friend that I would like to go into business with is... because...

I relate better one on one/in a crowd because...

I get along better with boys/girls because...

*My ideal "day
with a friend"
would be...*

The most valuable thing I have learned from a friend is...

My experience with "labeling" others or being labeled myself is...

I was
surprised
when I became
friends with...
because...

People who don't
know me might
describe me as...
because...

This is my personal advice about dating...

I will know I am ready to date seriously when...

Some things about dating that make me nervous are...   because...

It is/is not important to consider what my friends/family think about my girl/boyfriend because...

When I like someone, this is how I show it...

Dating would be easier if... because...

The 10 qualities I am looking for in a girl/boyfriend are...

My agenda for the perfect first date...

7:00 pm

8:00 pm

9:00 pm

10:00 pm

11:00 pm

12:00 midnight

If I knew I was leaving tomorrow, I would make sure these messages got to the following people.

person   message

These are the things I do to let someone know I care...

I know someone cares about me when...

You have just won a weekend at your favorite resort.
You can take one friend with you. Who would you take? Why?

You are being exiled to a deserted island for a week.
You can take one friend with you. Who would you take? Why?

past

We inherit from our ancestors gifts so often taken for granted...
Each of us contains within... this inheritance of soul.
~Edward Sellner

We learn from our past to positively influence our future. Our life stories help us understand where we are now and help lead us to the paths we might choose for our future. This chapter is designed to be a place for adolescents to explore their thoughts and emotions about past experiences, reflect on what they learned, and understand how it has shaped their lives.

- Use this chapter to celebrate the people who have been positive influences and role models. By identifying the people who have had an impact on us, we learn the value of nurturing these kinds of connections throughout our life.

- As your group explores the past, help them focus on the hope that knowing where we come from can help us shape where we are going.

- Quotes can be great prompts for inspiring reflective writing (see page 123). For additional quotes and some simple directions for using them as prompts, see page 174.

- Again, be sensitive around sharing answers and group discussions that arise out of the prompts or discussion. Painful past experiences can be very difficult to share, and establishing positive group norms is a must. Be prepared to refer a student to other resources in your agency or school if issues arise that are out of your scope to handle.

One of the most daring things I ever did when I was younger was...

This is the story of my first kiss...

My favorite childhood toy was...

When I was a child, one of my favorite things to do on a summer day was...

The earliest place/face I can remember...

As a child, I would pretend to be...

this involved...

If I could live one day of my life over because it was so incredible, I would pick...

If I could change one event in my past it would be...   because...

Some of the most beautiful sights
I have ever seen are...

Every time I smell...
I think of...

A memory I would like to erase is...
because...

My favorite holiday as a child was...   because...

A person from my past that I would like to reconnect with is...   because...

I remember getting into trouble for...

This is a list of the broken bones/scars I have and how they happened...

One of the scariest things that ever happened to me was...

A time when I could sense what was going to happen before it did was... and it made me feel...

If we could remember perfectly all of our past...

If we could not remember anything...

Amy Tan said, "Memory feeds imagination."
To me that means...

The most fun I ever had was...   because...

My first experience with death was...

**Compromises I have made...
and my feelings about that...**

This is what I know about the day I was born...

This is what was going on in the world when I was born...

As a child, I thought being a teenager would be...

...and this is how it is different than I expected...

 *story you never get tired of hearing/telling...*

The advantage of a bad memory is that one enjoys several times the same good things for the first time.
Friedrich Nietzsche

One memory I would like to be able to frame and hang on my wall is...

present

existing thoughts, feelings, and experiences ——— **8**

What we are today comes from our thoughts of yesterday,
and our present thoughts build our life of tomorrow:
Our life is the creation of our mind.

Buddha

Chapter eight helps adolescents celebrate who they are right now. Teachers/counselors will find these prompts invaluable for gauging the current mindset of their students/clients.

- This chapter can help adolescents get in touch with their feelings. Encourage them to stop, "take a moment," and contemplate their thoughts and reactions.

- These prompts can help students/clients focus on the reality of what is happening right now in their world. Some of these prompts can help them formulate a plan to take action.

- We borrowed the idea for "Today I am..." on page 136 from *Springboards: Quick Creative Activities to Launch Learning* (see resources on page 185):

    Activity Notes: This activity is more powerful than it first appears. The process of trying to figure out who you are turns out to be a challenge. Students often find that while the first few words come quickly, it becomes more and more difficult as the activity progresses for them to name the different parts of who they are.

- This chapter lends itself to including photography and artwork in the journaling process.

The most significant event happening in my life right now is...
and this is how it's affecting me...

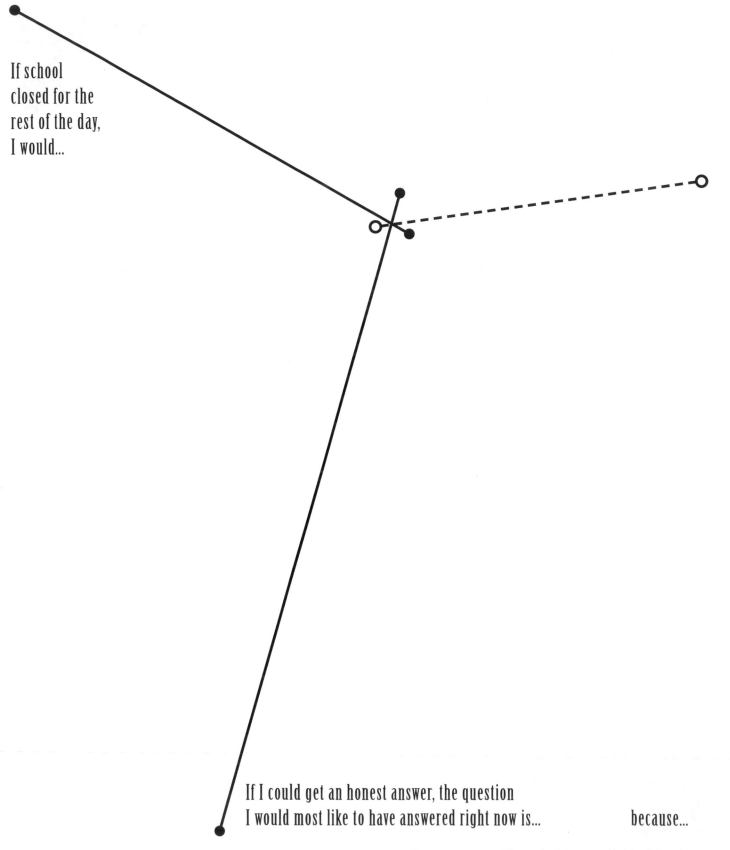

If school
closed for the
rest of the day,
I would...

If I could get an honest answer, the question
I would most like to have answered right now is...   because...

I think the most significant event happening in the world today is...
and this is how it's affecting me...

Today I am thankful for...

If I could change one thing about this day, it would be...

My goals for this day are...

I feel good about myself right
this minute because...

My frustrations/concerns at this
moment are...

It is "the first day of the rest of my life," and I am going to start fresh with...

If I was the opposite sex for the next 24 hours, I would...

A gift I would like to have waiting for me when I get home today is... because...

If I could change lives with someone else for the next 24 hours, it would be...
because...

This is what I have done today that I think is worth posting on Facebook...

All I really need right now is...

Some things that get me into trouble
these days are...

This is
what I think
of myself today...

Thinking about the
last few days, this is
what I could have
done better...

Today would be a great day if...

My day started out...

because...

By the time this day is over, I will...   because...

Lately, this is what motivates me to get out of bed...

The gifts I bring to the world today are...

Someone meeting me for the first time today might have this first impression...

"Yesterday is history, tomorrow is a mystery, today is a gift, that is why they call it the present." -unknown

because...

The soundtrack of my life...

A list of simple things I could do to make this a better day...

+
+
+
+
+
+
+
+
+
+
+
+

Today, I am...

How many different, one-word endings describe you?

Change is the law of life.
And those who look only to the past or present are certain to miss the future.

John F. Kennedy

This chapter provides the opportunity for students to ponder "what will be." Adolescents often hear what others want for them in the future. Parents, teachers, and guidance counselors often advise them to pursue paths such as college, military, sports, and extracurricular activities. This chapter allows students to reflect on how they see their future and take responsibility and ownership for creating their own path. These prompts range from what is happening next week to the distant future. Help students use them to understand the scope of the future and their ability to shape it one step at a time.

- Encourage students to "go big" when responding to these prompts and think of all of the possibilities.

- This a great chapter for helping adolescents set goals and make plans for next summer, next year, or for their professional future. The prompts on pages 139–141 will help encourage students to identify and access resources that will help them in planning and pursuing these goals.

- This is another chance to enforce the notion of being a change agent. "I can be a change agent, even though I'm not perfect and haven't yet arrived."

- Use these questions to jump-start discussions on how teens can impact not only their own future but also the future of their community and the world around them.

- Again, we borrowed the idea for "I want to be..." on page 152 from *Springboards: Quick Creative Activities to Launch Learning* (see resources on page 185):

    Activity Notes: This activity is more powerful than it first appears. The process of trying to figure out who you are turns out to be a challenge. Students often find that while the first few words come quickly, it becomes more and more difficult as the activity progresses for them to name the different parts of who they are.

When I think of the future, I wonder...

I want my next fortune cookie to say...

Some people that I hope will be part of my future are...

because...

The job I would like to have for this summer is...   because...

Some steps I can take toward getting that summer job are...

If all jobs in the future paid the same, I would want to...

because...

These are my thoughts on the importance of planning ahead for my future...

Resources I could be tapping right now to plan my future are...

Things that distract me from planning for my future are...   because...

Some of my goals for the future are...

To get where I want to be 10 years from now, these are the steps I need to take...

Some research I have done toward planning my future...   because...

Changes I think I will see in my community as time passes are...

I would someday like to impact my community by...

If I could choose to know the future... because...

I think tomorrow will be better/worse than today because...

Some things I think I will miss most about being a kid are... because...

When I think about being on my own, I get excited about...

The person who has most influenced my future is...   because...

Someday I hope to live...   because...

My definition of "destiny" is...

Responsibilities I look forward
to assuming are...

When time travel becomes possible, the first
place I want to go is...   because...

Some of my concerns about the future are...

This is how I think family structure will change in the future...

This is how I see life changing if the world runs out of water...

If I have the chance to travel into space, I will...   because...

This is how I want people to remember me...

If I could take only one possession into the future with me, it would be... because...

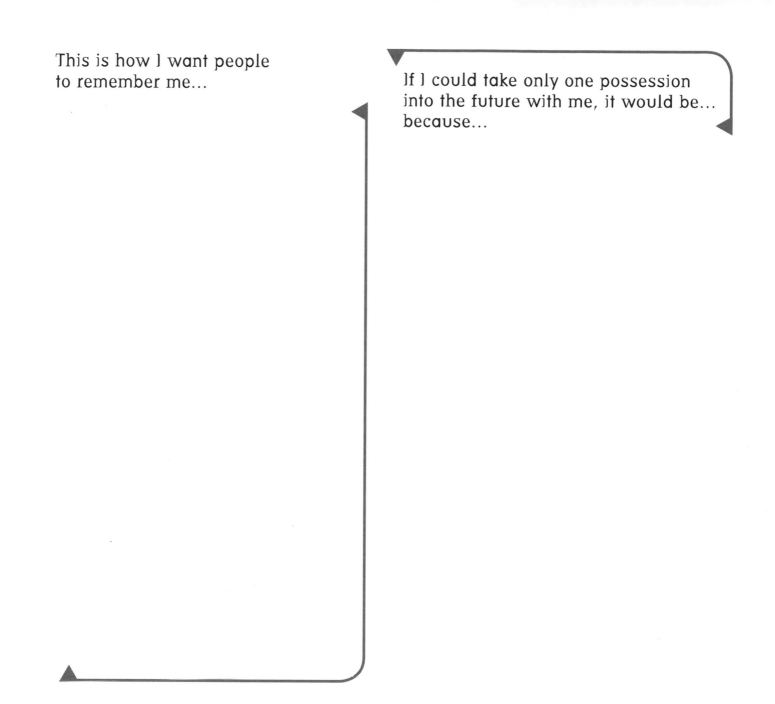

Fifty years from now, I will know I had a successful life if...

These are my thoughts about getting old...
because...

My thoughts on how
medical advancements
might change my life...

My plans for leaving the world a lasting monument would be...   because...

The highest level of education I hope to attain is...   because...

When I
finish school,
I hope to live...

My dream career
would be...

10 pieces of advice I would like to pass on to myself to read in the future are...

1.

2.

3.

4.

5.

6.

7.

8.

9.

10.

10 places I hope to visit in my lifetime are

1
2
3
4
5
6
7
8
9
10

10 things I hope to accomplish in my lifetime are

1
2
3
4
5
6
7
8
9
10

I want to be...

How many different, one- or two-word endings describe you?

—— brainstorming, considering all the possibilities, prioritizing, and reminders ——

Lists can be used in a number of ways. A list is not limited to 10 items—add or subtract more as needed. Lists can contain items that have a ranking where the number-one item is the most important or all the items on the list can have equal value. Lists can also change, so revisit them from time to time to update your preferences.

The list prompt, Things I Never Want to Forget, on page 158 can be a way to pull it all together. Ask your students to identify the things they want to remember from this journaling experience— key learnings, reflections, and insights they never want to forget.

Top 10....

Things I would like to buy when I have money.

Movies I've seen.

Vacation spots.

Foods I always want in my house.

Movie stars I'd like to meet.

Ways to spend 24 hours.

Toppings I would put on a pizza.

Television shows.

Restaurants I hope never close.

Things I would put between two pieces of bread.

Sweet-tooth foods.

Places I would like to hike.

Things I would do with $50 ($500 total for all items).

Items that should always be 50% off retail price.

Olympic sports I enjoy watching.

Animated characters.

Places I like to shop.

Websites on my favorites list.

Electronics I would like to have in my life.

Places to read a book.

Reasons I have for getting a driver's license.

Things I lose.

DVDs I would save forever.

Icecream toppings.

People I text regularly.

People who frequent my Facebook.

People I have on speed dial.

Teachers I've had in my life so far.

Games to play on road trips.

Games to play that don't require electronics.

Crazy things I've done in my life.

Reasons for having a pet.

Things to do backwards.

T-shirt slogans.

Things I will never do in my lifetime.

Days in my life so far.

Cartoon characters I'd like to see brought back.

Cartoon characters I'd like to see canceled.

Movie heroes.

Reasons to have a cell phone.

Halloween costumes.

Must haves for Thanksgiving dinner.

Ways to exercise.

People I would invite to my next party.

Top 10....

Songs I like to listen to.

Ways to make friends.

Acts of kindness I've done in my lifetime.

Quotes to remember.

Pieces of information I want to remember from school so far.

Ways to keep friends.

Things I think about on a regular basis.

Things my parents want me to remember.

Reasons to stay in school.

Reasons to go to college.

Universities I would apply to.

Jobs I would like to choose from in my lifetime.

Causes I would give money to.

Books I will always have on my shelf.

Words that mean a lot to me.

Things that will never stay the same.

Things I wish I could do over.

Famous people I would like to talk with.

Things I would want with me if I were deserted on an island.

Characteristics I want my friends to remember me by.

Adjectives that describe me at this time.

Things I could do to be more responsible.

Things I could do to be more carefree.

Things I could do to make the world a better place.

Things I would like to have invented.

Things that need to be invented.

Reasons why people take pictures.

Things I don't want to do around the house.

Accomplishments I've achieved so far.

Things I could do to help out my parents.

Things I can start today to ensure my future is rewarding.

Reasons to dress up.

Composers of all time.

Reasons for having to be quiet.

Ways to be nice to someone.

Smells I enjoy.

Things I treasure.

Characteristics that make me unique.

Favors I can give away.

Daydreams.

Things I enjoy doing.

Things I am curious about.

Things I enjoy hearing.

Things I like to see.

Reasons to give up complaining.

Comfort foods.

Things to do in a group.

Things to do alone.

Topics of conversation.

Opportunities I don't want to miss.

Successes of my life so far.

Reasons to live.

Essentials for a good life.

Things to consider when discouraged.

Fears.

Things closest to my heart.

Reasons to recycle.

Things that bug me.

Questions I would like to be asked.

Questions I would like to ask.

Reasons to journal.

TOP 10 ADVENTURES I WANT TO PARTICIPATE IN...

Fun things I can do for free...

"IT IS BETTER TO KNOW SOME OF THE QUESTIONS THAN ALL OF THE ANSWERS." —JAMES THURBER

Things I never want to forget...

make it personal

— blank prompt templates and more questions

Every individual matters. Every individual has a role to play. Every individual makes a difference.

Jane Goodall

The following blank templates are provided for those times when you want to make up your own prompts to focus on a particular topic or move in a specific direction. They can also be used as blank worksheet for participants to fill in with their own prompts/thoughts, or with prompts decided on by the group. Jen Stanchfield has found that many educators find the blank templates perfect for creating their own reflection worksheets with a focus on a specific lesson or reflective theme. Jen shares the following specific examples from her work with educators in the field—one from a 7th grade language arts class and one from a 6th grade guidance group.

7th Grade Language Arts Poetry Unit Example

To jumpstart a lesson on poetry with 7th grade students, the following questions were added to a blank prompt template from *The Me I See* to help students explore their prior experiences with poetry through music.

> Think of a song you love, or that you remember the words to.
> What song is it? Who performed it? Describe the song.
>
> What is it you like about this song?
>
> Why did it leave such an impression on you? Why do you remember the verses?

This worksheet was used as an entry task at the start of day one of our poetry unit. After students completed the reflective writing, they shared in small groups. We found this entry task helped them buy into the poetry lesson and engage in a larger group discussion.

Strengths Reflection for School Community Building Example

As part of an ongoing focus at Twin Valley Middle School to build a positive school climate, 6th grade students were encouraged to reflect on their personal strengths and how those strengths contribute to the greater school community. To begin the project, a reflection page with the following prompts was created to inspire students' thoughts around their personal strengths.

> Three of my personal strengths are...
>
> These personal strengths are important to me and my community/society because...
>
> I demonstrate these personal strengths every day by...

After completing this reflective writing, the students shared first in small groups and then with the larger group about their personal strengths. This combination of personal reflection combined with group discussion was found to increase the students' understanding of what a personal strength was, and it gave them an opportunity to give and receive positive feedback from their peers about their strengths.

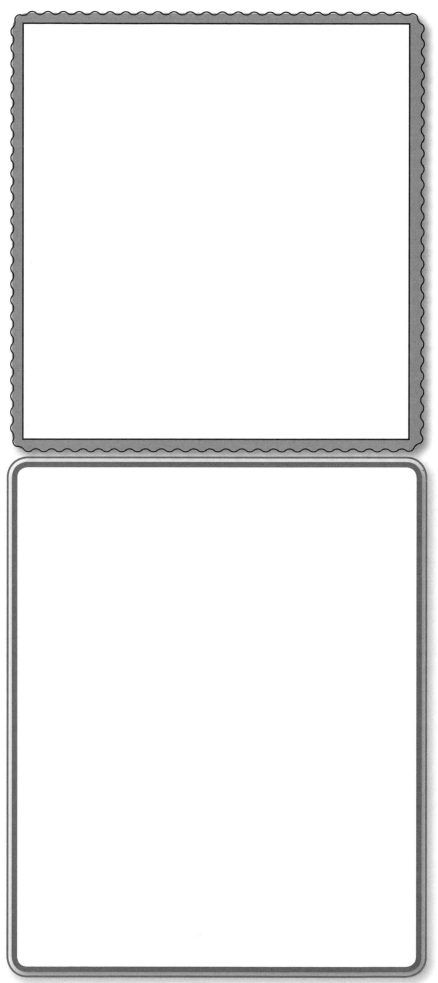

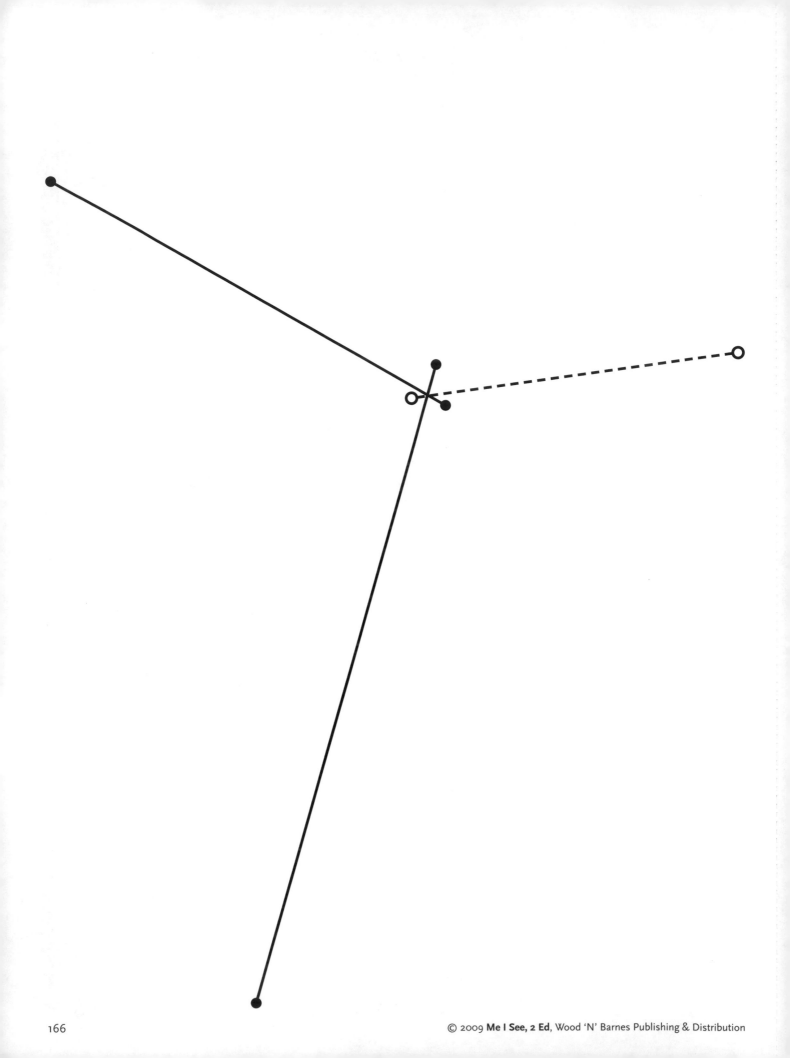

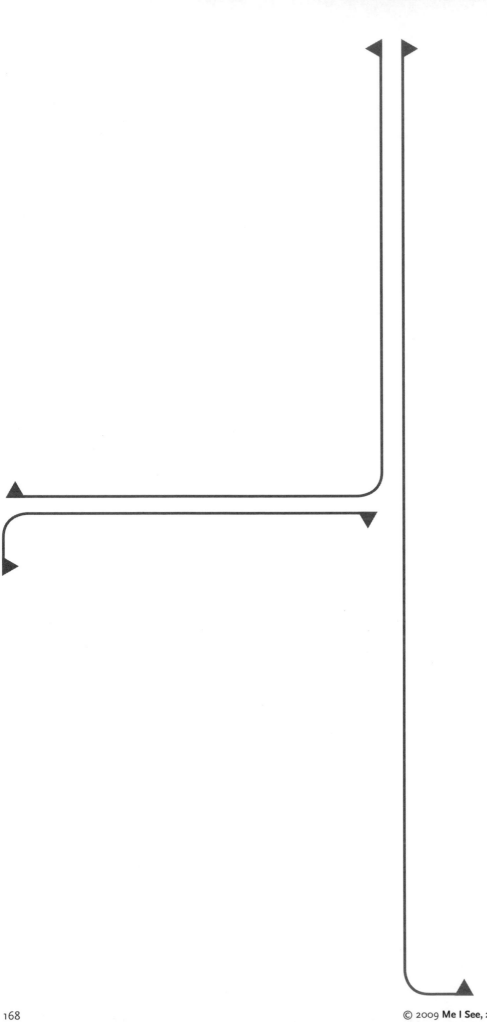

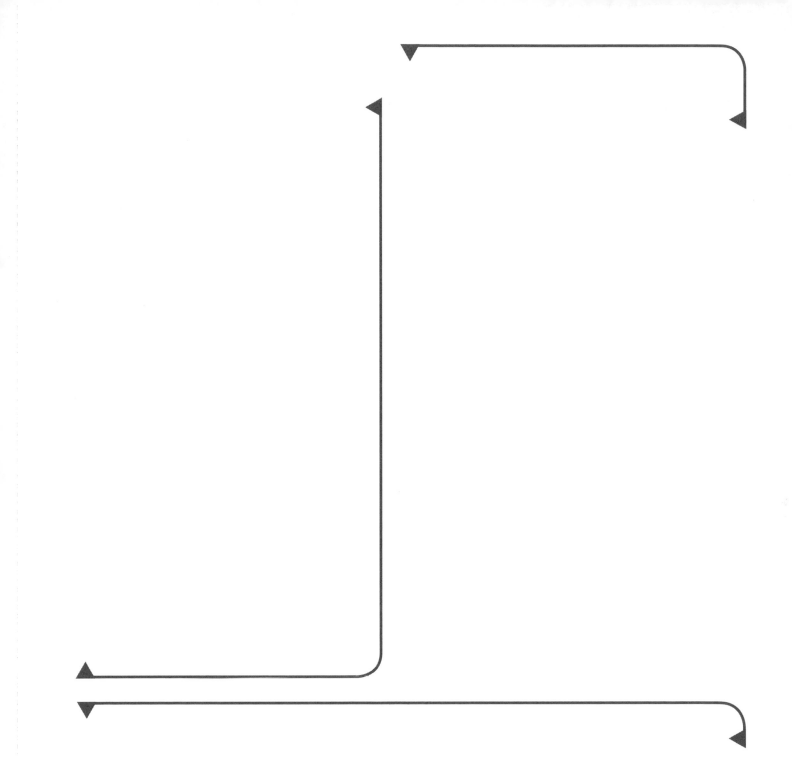

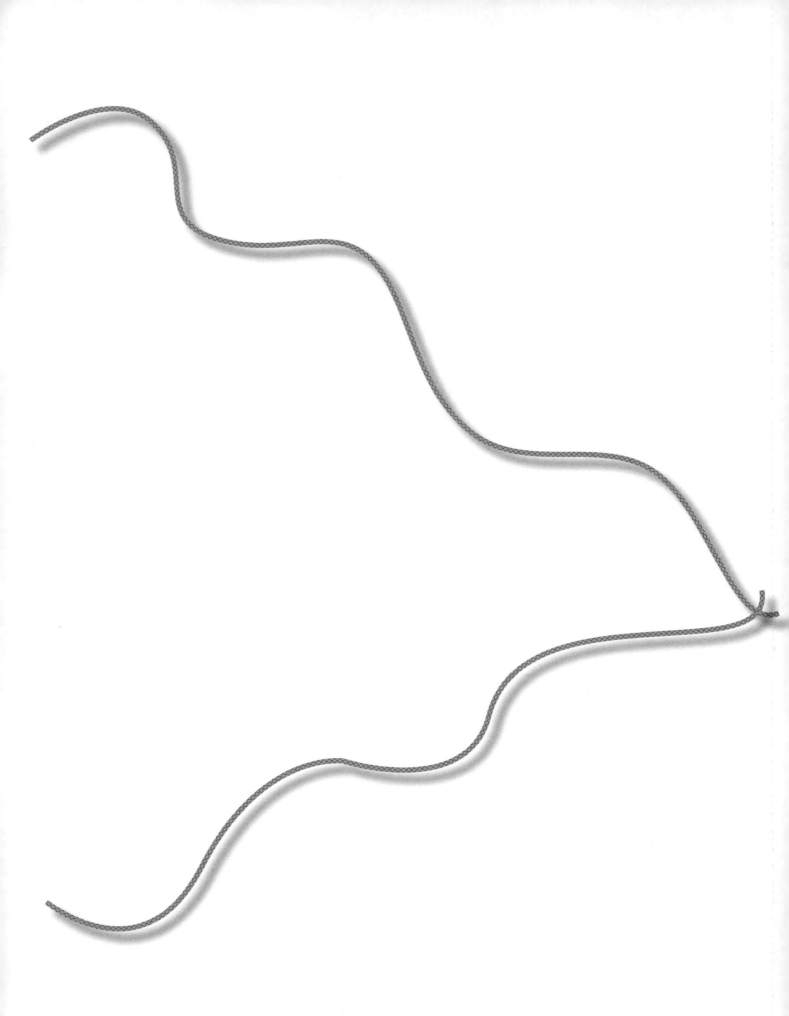

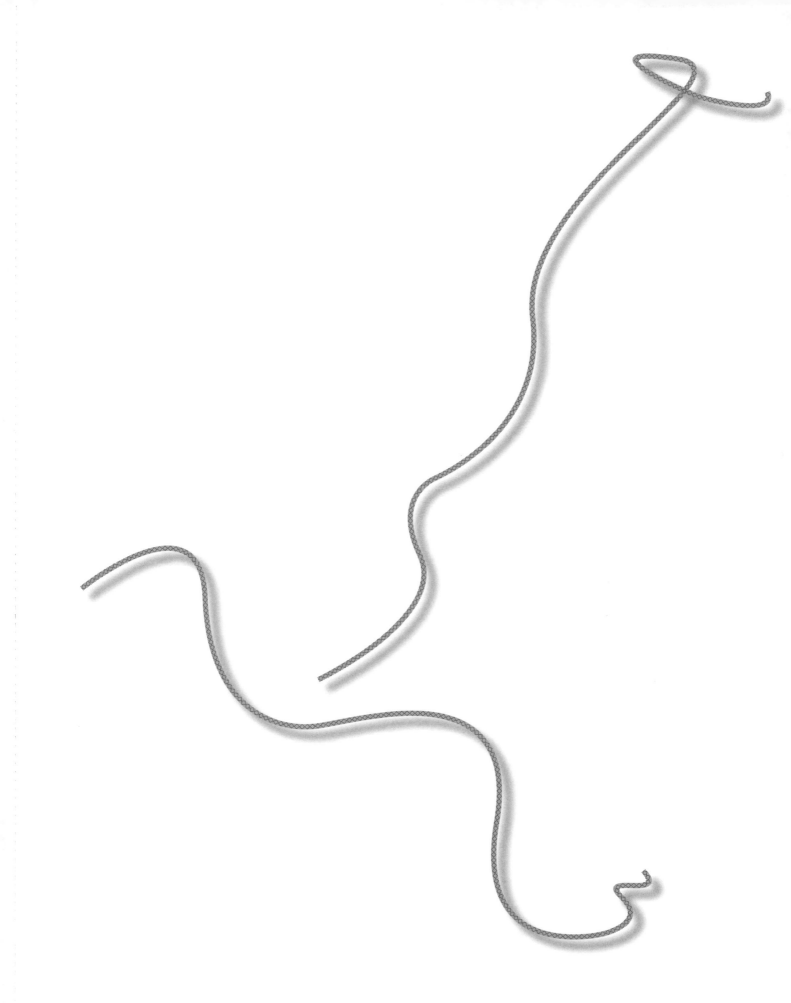

quote prompts

— **inspirational words to spark reflective writing**

We got the idea to include a few quotes for prompts from Leslie Rapparlie. Her example of using a quote as a prompt for leadership was:

Quote: *If you're a leader, a fellow that other fellows look to, you've got to keep going.*
         ~Ernest Shackleton

Prompt: This quote makes me think about...

         OR pose a question/concept after the quote, like:

         Describe a difficult time you experienced as a leader and how you "kept going"...

Other quotes ideas:

Nobody can go back and start a new beginning, but anyone can start today and make a new ending.
~Maria Robinson

The family. We were a strange little band of characters trudging through life sharing diseases and toothpaste, coveting one another's desserts, hiding shampoo, borrowing money, locking each other out of our rooms, inflicting pain and kissing to heal it in the same instant, loving, laughing, defending, and trying to figure out the common thread that bound us all together. ~Erma Bombeck

The past is a good place to visit, but I wouldn't want to live there. ~Author Unknown

Don't let yesterday use up too much of today. ~Cherokee Indian Proverb

Life's a journey, not a destination. ~Aerosmith

The best thing about the future is that it comes only one day at a time. ~Abraham Lincoln

There are people who have money and people who are rich. ~Coco Chanel

Most men are more capable of great actions than of good ones. ~Montesquieu, Variètès

The only time you realize you have a reputation is when you are not living up to it. ~Jose Iturbi

Sometimes you put walls up not to keep people out, but to see who cares enough to break them down.
~unknown

Promise me you'll always remember: You're braver than you believe, and stronger than you seem, and smarter than you think. ~Christopher Robin to Pooh

A friend is someone who understands your past, believes in your future, and accepts you just the way you are. ~unknown

Sport is a very important subject at school, that's why I gave Quidditch such an important place at Hogwarts. I was very bad in sports, so I gave Harry a talent I would really loved to have. Who wouldn't want to fly? ~Joanne Kathleen Rowling

Chapter 1: The Me I See — personal insights, feelings, and motives

My favorite spectator sports are... because...

If I ever have the opportunity to design a house that reflects my personality, it will include...

My favorite kind of music is... because...

Some of my favorite musical groups are... because...

The style of music that best fits my life right now is... because...

My favorite comic book or animated character is... because...

If I were the star of a television show, I would want my role to be... because...

My favorite season of the year is... because...

My favorite holiday is... because...

The color that best describes me is... because...

If I could choose any animal for a pet it would be... because...

I am strangely attracted to... because...

You have my undivided attention when...

Some people think my sense of humor is...

If the story of my life were made into a novel, the title would be... because...

These are some of the names of the chapters in my life so far...

These are some of the coauthors of the current chapters in my life...

These are some possible names for future chapters in my life...

My favorite fairy tale is... because...

I am a "leader" rather than a "follower" when...

I am a "follower" rather than a "leader" when...

If I could change one physical characteristic, it would be...

If I knew I had one week to live...

An animal I would like to come face to face with is... because...

Sometimes, I just have to... because...

I hope I never have to... because...

These are the best things about being a boy/girl... because...

I am not a very good cook when it comes to...

If I could live one year of my life over again...

These are some things I choose to say "NO" to...

These are some of the things I choose to say "YES" to...

Some habits I have that are good for me include...

If it was possible to program my dreams, tonight I would like to dream about...

The most controlling person in my life is...

One secret I have held on to for years and never told anybody is...

Some of the biggest lies I ever told were... and the reason I told them was...

Answering these questions today has...

Chapter 2: Values — identifying, clarifying, and understanding beliefs

My Twitter feed would say...

The possession I have that most defines me is... because...

Sometimes, I get too preoccupied with...

A person from the past that I would like to trade places with is... because...

This is how my beliefs affect my life...

Some things that I do differently because of my beliefs are...

Things I know to be true are... and how I learned them...

Things I know to be false are... and how I learned them...

This is how (and why) my present beliefs are different from those I was raised with...

This is my definition of "prayer"...

This is how I define "God"...

This is how I think God sees me...

I do/do not believe in God because...

The role of spirituality in my life today...

These are my thoughts on religion in general...

I find myself getting confused by religion when...

I wonder about the existence of God or a higher power when...

A note I would like to write to God is...

These are my thoughts on creation...

These are my thoughts on Darwin's theory of evolution...

My religious heritage includes... and this is how I feel about it...

These are my thoughts on angels and other spirits...

My personal experience around interacting with those of other faiths is...

I would/would not marry someone of another faith because...

My personal thoughts about atheism are...

This is what "freedom of religion" means to me...

If I could give a year of my life to help others, I would...

A pilgrimage I would like to make is... because...

A volunteer organization I would like to be part of is... because...

Some of my most sincere prayers and wishes...

The person or event having the most impact on my spirituality is...

I think paying taxes on the money I earn is... because...

I lie about things because...

This is what I think about smoking...

My personal thought on using drugs and alcohol...

The first time I was offered a cigarette, I...

The first time I was offered marijuana or another drug was... and this is what happened...

My personal experience with shoplifting is...

My definition of a "soul mate" is...

My thoughts on marriage are...

This is how I feel about spending my entire lifetime with just one person... because...

These are my thoughts on living together before marriage...

These are my views on premarital sex...

My thoughts on divorce are...

I think the ideal wedding would include...

These are my thoughts on having children...

These are my thoughts on adopting a child...

The first time I learned that a friend/acquaintance my age had sex was... and this is how I felt when I heard about it...

The first time I found out a friend/acquaintance of mine was pregnant I felt...

If I found out today that I was pregnant or had made someone pregnant I would...

This is how I feel about abortion...

This is what I would say to a friend who was thinking about an abortion...

These are my personal thoughts/experiences with sexually transmitted diseases...

I think sexually transmitted diseases can/cannot be prevented because...

This is what I think about birth control...

When I find out someone that I know is HIV positive or has AIDS, I...

My personal thoughts about homosexuality are...

Juveniles are often tried as adults for crimes such as rape or murder. These are my thoughts on the issue and why I think this way...

This is what I would die for...

When I die, I would/would not like to donate my organs to others because...

If I knew I had one week to live, I...

This is where and how I would like to die...

These are my thoughts about suicide...

These are my thoughts about doctor-assisted suicide...

If I found out a friend was considering suicide, I would...

This is what I think life after death is going to be like...

Chapter 3: Views — observations on the world around me

The ideal presidential candidate would have these qualities...

If I were president, I would choose these people to be members of my cabinet...

If I owned a television station, I would...

Texting is/is not important to me because...

These are my thoughts on sexting...

I find the Internet to be...

I would recommend Facebook or MySpace pages because....

These are some ways the Internet has changed the world for the better...

These are some ways the Internet has harmed today's world...

I don't use e-mail or texting to communicate with my friends when...

I feel/don't feel safe expressing myself through technology, like e-mails, because...

This is how I feel about global warming... and what I can do about it...

My thoughts on saving trees are... because...

This is what I think about animal protection activism...

These are my thoughts on riding a bicycle instead of driving a car to school/work... because...

These are my thoughts on volunteering my time to those in need... because...

This is something I do to help out in my community...

These are some things I have done to help someone in need...

As for the possibilities of life on other planets, I tend to think...

This is how I feel about politics and politicians...

This is how I feel about being able to vote... because...

I do not respect people in authority when...

This is the first thing I would do about unemployment... because...

These are my thoughts on the racial issues in our country...

I believe that opportunities are/are not equal for males and females.... because...

In an ideal society, this is the place I would create for our elderly... because...

These are my ideas on how to take care of the homeless...

These are my thoughts about cloning animals/human beings...

These are some of the ways I feel the fashion industry affects me and everyone around me...

Some of my thoughts on plastic surgery are...

This is what I think about pornography...

These are the immigration laws I would support... because...

My personal experiences with eating disorders such as anorexia and bulimia...

My thoughts on dieting include...

Chapter 4: Family — family history, development, experiences, and influences

The best family vacation/holiday we ever had...

This is what my family does for birthdays...

Some of the pets we had as a family were...

The one thing we would all agree to eat for a family dinner is...

Some of my first memories of grandparents are...

Being around my grandparents is...

If I could take my family any place I wanted for vacation, I would...

These are some fond memories I have about my father...

These are some fond memories I have about my mother...

The fairy tale characters my parents most remind me of are... because...

This is what you would learn about my family by looking in our refrigerator...

This is a description of a typical evening at my house...

Our favorite television show we watch together as a family is... because...

This is how I feel about my siblings/being an only child...

These are some good things my parents are doing, that I will want to do when I am a parent...

This is something I learned from a family member recently...

As a child, these where some of the things that got me into trouble the most...

If I could change something about my family, it would be...

Some things my parents have done that I am going to do differently are...

When I am a parent, this is how I will discipline my children...

The stupidest/best rules I've had to follow while growing up have been...

Things my parents never told me, but I would really like to hear...

This is what I would like to say to my father...

This is what I would like to say to my mother...

This is what my parents taught me about drinking alcohol...

This is what my parents taught me about smoking...

This is what my parents taught me about drugs...

This is what I wish my parents had said when they first talked to me about drugs...

When my parents get angry with each other, they...

When my parents are angry with me, they...

My parents' attitude toward life seems to be...

These are my thoughts about my parents choice in friends...

My family is addicted to...

This is how I am like my father...

This is how I am like my mother...

This is my definition of "family loyalty"...

The worst time I ever experienced with my parents was when...

The worst time I ever spent with relatives was when...

The last time we had a family discussion, it was about...

I do not enjoy... with my family, because...

The most controlling person in my family is... and this is how it affects me...

The most reliable person in my family is... because...

My family's idea of punishment is...

My family's idea of reward is...

If I knew that I would never see my family again, this is what would I say to each one before I left...

This is what I hope my family will be like some day...

If someone that I loved was diagnosed with a terminal illness, this is what I think I would do...

Some things my family avoids talking about... I think it is because...

Chapter 5: School — educational pursuits and experiences

My personal expectations for my family to attend school events are... because...

I know I'm in a good school because...

The school subjects that seem the most pointless are... because...

The school subjects that seem the most valuable are... because...

One special moment that stands out in my mind about school is...

This is a list of teams, clubs, and other organizations that I am glad I was a part of because...

At school, there is/is not pressure to conform to certain stereotypes... because...

These are my thoughts about being required to learn a second language in school...

In school situations, I am a "follower" rather than a "leader" when...

In school situations, I tend to be a "leader" rather than a "follower" when...

If I decide not to go to college, here is what I plan to do...

My worst memories of school include...

Being in the "right" group at school is... because...

The worst punishment I ever received at school was...

One of the most destructive things a teacher ever said or did to me was...

School would be more useful and interesting to me if...

This is how I feel about walking to school, instead of taking the bus...

This is a description of my worst teacher ever...

In school, my worst class ever has been... because...

Chapter 6: Social — relationships, peer interaction, and community

This is the kind of friend I am...

This is my definition of "friend"...

My idea of a party includes...

This is an "ode" to a friend...

When I have extra money I like to share it with my friends by...

I would rather my friends come to my house/go to my friends' house because...

I hide things like... from my friends because...

This is about a time I defended a friend...

This is about a time when I upset a friend...

My friends would say that I'm...

Sometimes I have problems making friends because...

I think some people don't like me because...

I think three is company/a crowd because...

This is what I do when I see someone else getting picked on...

Some unlikely people I can remember having a crush on...

These are some memories about my very first romance...

When it comes to the subject of dating, my parents seem to feel...

This is how I feel about asking someone out on a date...

This is what I'd say to my date to help him/her feel comfortable...

The best date I've ever been on went like this...

This is what I do to get ready for a date...

If a friend/date made fun of me in front of others, I would...

I think the worst way to break up with someone is...

A time when I was unfaithful to someone I cared about was... and this was the result...

These are some of the advantages/disadvantages of staying single...

These are some of the advantages/disadvantages of getting married...

These are some of the people I would like to have around me when I'm older...

This is a list of people who depend on me...

This is what I would say to a friend who was thinking about taking drugs...

If I found out a friend was abusing (or addicted to) drugs or alcohol, I would...

This is someone I have enjoyed spending time with and this is what I've learned from him/her...

An older person I am close to is... because...

One of the most embarrassing things that ever happened to me was...

Communicating with older people is... because...

This is a thank-you note to someone who deserves it...

I do/do not consider myself a gossip because...

Some ways to respond to gossip are...

I like to gossip about... because...

I feel bad about gossip when...

If someone was talking about me behind my back, I would/would not want to know about it because...

These are some of the positive effects peer pressure has on me...

These are some of the negative effects peer pressure has on me...

My thoughts about fitting into the right crowd are...

I exclude some people from my social circle because...

I deal with people who are verbally or physically abusive to me by...

Chapter 7: Past — personal history and prior experiences

If I had a total, perfect memory of my past...

When I was a younger, I thought life at my present age would be...

These are some things I've done to make other people happy...

The most fun I ever had was...

I recall the first book ever read to me was...

When I was younger, the things I enjoyed collecting included...

When I was younger, these are some of the things I did on rainy days...

When I was younger, I wanted to grow up to be...

My best memories from school are...

Some of the best ideas I have ever had include...

The longest trip I ever took was...

My favorite trip or vacation was...

The smells that I connect with at home are...

This is a person who has influenced me in the past, and the reasons why...

As a child, my favorite hiding places were... I would go there when...

It took real courage for me to...

 © 2009 **Me I See, 2 Ed**, Wood 'N' Barnes Publishing & Distribution

One special moment that stands out in my mind is...

The best gift I ever received was...

When I got angry as a child, I...

One of the biggest mistakes I ever made was...

I wonder how my life would have turned out differently if...

These are some of the most rebellious things I have ever done...

The sickest I ever felt was...

A time in my life when I really could have used some counseling was...

My most memorable encounter with a police officer was...

Sometimes I feel guilty about...

The greatest heartbreak in my life came when...

I learned the truth about sex from...

A secret I have held on to for years is...

The worst pain I ever saw someone else in was... It made me feel...

I was raised to deal with physical pain by...

My experiences with hospitals include...

My first experience with death was... and this is what I learned...

My first friend/acquaintance that died was... and this is how I felt...

When I was younger, I made a stand when it came to...

I feel I was abused or taken advantage of as a child when...

These are some compromises I have made so far in my life and why I had to make them...

The time in my life that I cried the most was...

Some of the biggest lies I ever told were... and the reason I told them was...

Chapter 8: Present — existing thoughts, feelings, and experiences

This is what someone might learn about me from the way I am dressed today...

The TV shows I'll be watching this week are... because...

Right now, I would like to text... and ask him/her...

If I could access only one Website on my computer today, it would be... because...

If it rains over the weekend, this is what I'll be doing....

Lately, I have been dreaming about...

These are some tasks I would like to get done by the end of this week...

Sit back... relax... daydream...

My wants at this moment are...

Something I feel guilty about today is...

Something that made me really angry recently was...

The last time I felt disappointed in someone was... because...

If I could be somewhere else at this moment, it would be...

The best thing about today is...

Chapter 9: Future — goals, hopes, plans, dreams, and possibilities

This is the last big vacation I would like to take before I start my career...

This is the sport I would like to excel at in the near future...

If I could be anywhere next year, I would choose to be... because...

If I met the President tomorrow, this is what I would ask him...

This is where I would live outside of the United States...

This is where I hope to live when I have a family...

In the future, I really don't see myself doing...

The ideal age to get married would be... because...

This is what I hope my family will be like some day...

This is how I think the world might work without a money system...

These are some possible names for future chapters in my life...

This is how I think transportation will change in the future...

The ideal government structure for the future would be...

I think the role of religion in the future will...

I think that if I ever go into business for myself, it would be...

By the time I am 40, I hope my life will be...

Diseases that will be cured in my lifetime are...

This is how I think computer technology will continue to change in the future...

I think sharing our planet with other forms of life would be... because...

This is the age I would like to retire and what I plan to be doing...

If I could take a pill that would make me immortal...

One thing I would like to do while I am still young is... because...

I would like my epitaph to read...

If I could choose my own ending, this is the age and where and how I want to die...

When I die, this is what I'd like for my family and friends to do...

resources

Group Facilitation and Creating a Positive Environment for Sharing

Changing the Message by Jeff Albin, 2004. Wood 'N' Barnes Publishing, Bethany, OK.
Ideas for working on prevention with groups.

Journey Toward the Caring Classroom by Laurie Frank, 2004. Wood 'N' Barnes Publishing, Bethany, OK.
Ideas for creating a positive environment for sharing in the classroom.

Open to Outcome: A Practical Guide for Facilitating & Teaching Experiential Reflection by Micah Jacobsen and Mari Ruddy, 2004. Wood 'N' Barnes Publishing, Bethany, OK.
A model for peer mentoring and using reflective questions with groups of teens.

Tips & Tools: The Art of Experiential Group Facilitation by Jennifer Stanchfield, 2007. Wood 'N' Barnes Publishing, Bethany, OK.
Facilitation tips and ideas for creating a positive environment for sharing in the classroom and group work setting.

Writing and Journaling

The Artist's Way by Julie Cameron, 1992. Putnam Books, New York.

Classroom Assessment Techniques by Angelo & Cross, 1993. Jossey Bass, San Francisco, CA.

Engaging Ideas: The Professors Guide to Integrating Writing, Critical Thinking, and Active Learning in the Classroom by John C Bean, 1996. Jossey Bass, San Francisco, CA.

The Journal Book by T. Fulwiler, 1987. Heinemann Books, Portsmouth, NH.

Teaching With Writing, edited by Toby Fulwiler, 1986. The University of Vermont, Boynton Cook.

Write to Learn: A Guide to Writing Across the Curriculum by Soven, 1996. South-Western College Publishing, Cincinnati, OH.

The Writer's Toolbox by Brown, Roen & Mittan, 1997. Allyn & Bacon Publisher, Needham Heights, MA.

Writing Down the Bones: Freeing the Writer Within by Natalie Goldberg, 1986. Shambhala Publications, Boston, MA.

Writing to Change the World by Mary Pipher, 2006. Riverhead Books/Penguin Group, New York.

Questions

If Anybody Asks Me: 1001 Questions for Educators, Counselors, & Therapists, Larry Eckerd, 1998. Wood 'N' Barnes Publishing, Bethany, OK.
Another great resource for questions.

What Would It Be Like.../Are You More Like...: A Back-to-Back Book of Anytime Questions for Anysize Answers by Chris Cavert and Susana Acosta Cavert, 2006. Wood 'N' Barnes Publishing, Bethany, OK. *Great questions for initiating reflection and group discussion.*